BIRMINGHAM IN THE FORTIES

Alton & Jo Douglas

The Onion Fair, under construction, Serpentine Ground, Aston, 28th September 1949.

© 2000 Alton and Jo Douglas
ISBN 1 85858 171 0
Published by Brewin Books Ltd., Doric House, 56 Alcester Road, Studley, Warwickshire B80 7LG.
Printed by Warwick Printing Co. Ltd., Theatre Street, Warwick CV34 4DR.
Layout by Alton and Jo Douglas

Preparations are underway for the Royal visit the following week, Council House, 8th May 1948.

Front Cover: The official last tram, on the Ladywood route, waits to pull out from Navigation Street,
1st September 1947.

C o n t e n t s

BREWIN BOOKS LTD

Doric House, 56 Alcester Road,
Studley, Warwickshire B80 7LG

Tel: 01527 854228 Fax: 01527 852746

Vat Registration No. 705 0077 73

Dear Nostalgic,

One little niggle, at the back of my mind, when we set out on this adventure was that, having produced three books on the city during the Second World War, ("Birmingham at War Vol 1", "Birmingham at War Vol 2" and "Birmingham: The War Years") and several titles that included items from those eventful years, there might be a shortage of material. I reckoned, foolishly, without your help – in the end we finished up with enough rare items to fill the deepest bomb crater! So, in your hands, you now have a scrapbook packed to the gunnels (that's quite enough wartime images for one brief intro!) with material that takes us up to the end of the war and then into those difficult, challenging years that lay immediately afterwards. Has there ever been such an engrossing period in our city's history? I think not.

Yours, in friendship,

Alton

Digbeth, 26th June 1949.

Keys make salvage
Birmingham has begun a drive for old, unwanted keys for salvage.

Stacking aluminium pots and pans, for use in the manufacture of fighter planes, 1940.

Your kitchen range must burn _less_ this winter !

Get to know it better. Persuade it to do more — for less! Every scuttle saved means more for the factories, to swell the output of weapons — to finish the job.

ECONOMISE IN EVERY WAY YOU CAN

Here are some examples:

Have a fire in one room only—breakfast in the kitchen	Wrap up hot water pipes and tanks to retain heat
Never use your oven for a single dish	Waste occurs when dampers are open unnecessarily
Use less hot water for baths and washing up	Sift and use all cinders, and use coal dust for banking

Call at your Coal Office or Gas or Electricity Showroom for advice and leaflets on how to economise.

Save FUEL for the factories
All Fuels are equally important

COAL · COKE · GAS · ELECTRICITY · FUEL OIL · PARAFFIN

ISSUED BY THE MINES DEPARTMENT

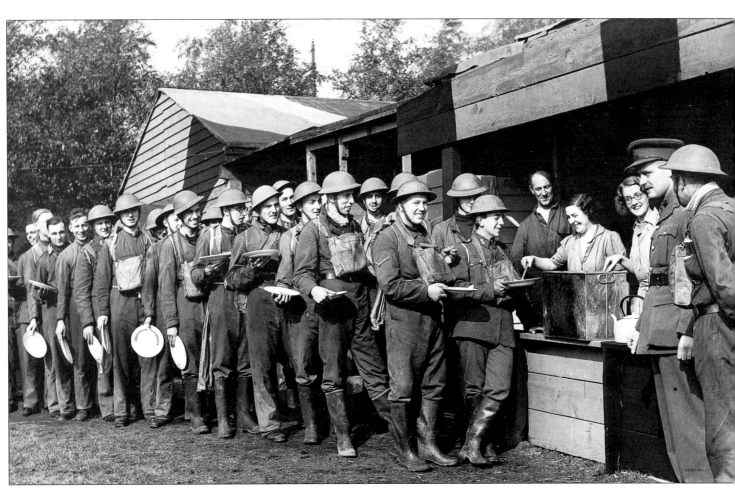

Grub up! An Anti-Aircraft Station, c 1940.

Dignitaries at the opening of the Maternity and Child Welfare Centre, Tower Hill, Perry Barr, 5th March 1940.

Local Defence Volunteers (shortly to become the Home Guard) shoulder arms, May 1940.

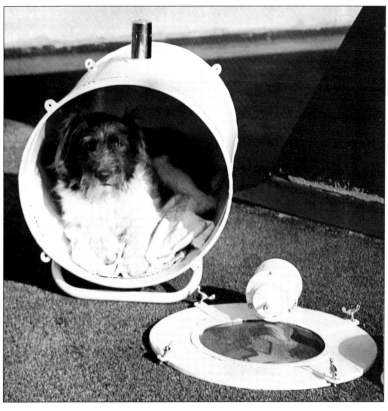

A gas-proof kennel, 1940.

5

WORKS WONDERS FOR A·R·P WORKERS

TO OVERCOME FAINTNESS

Lift the Stopper and Sniff

ARP (Air Raid Precaution) Wardens, May 1940.

Austin Street, Nechells, 1940.

TILES BROKEN & DISPLACED BY BLAST

GARAGE & SHEDS COMPLETELY WRECKED

ALL WINDOWS SHATTERED

ANDERSON SHELTER INTACT & OCCUPANTS UNHURT THOUGH NEARER TO BOMB THAN HOUSES

CRATER MADE BY MEDIUM BOMB

SPORT can generally find the best answer to the Dismal Jimmies of the world. In a letter to the "Times" Mr. Victor Hely-Hutchinson, writing from Birmingham, says: "I believe that the following true story accurately represents the spirit of England at the moment.

"Yesterday evening the landlord of a public-house in Birmingham observed to a workman, whom he was serving with a drink, that the war news was pretty bad.' 'Oh, I don't know, was the answer, 'after all, it's the final, and we're playing it on our home ground.'"

RESIGNATION OF MR. CHAMBERLAIN. Confidence in the Government led by Mr. Chamberlain was seriously undermined by the general conduct of the war, and after a debate on the question in the Commons on 8 May, Mr. Chamberlain invited the Opposition to serve under him in a reconstructed Cabinet. Labour, however, refused and on 10 May the Premier resigned and was succeeded by Mr. Winston Churchill. Above is seen the new Premier together with some of the new Ministers. The new War Cabinet consisted of the Premier, who also became Minister of Defence; Mr. Chamberlain, Lord President of the Council; Lord Halifax, Foreign Secretary; Mr. C. R. Attlee, Lord Privy Seal, and Mr. Arthur Greenwood, Minister without Portfolio. Other Ministers were: Mr. A. V. Alexander, Admiralty; Mr. Anthony Eden, War; Sir Archibald Sinclair, Air; Sir John Simon, Lord Chancellor; Sir Kingsley Wood, Exchequer; Sir John Anderson, Home Secretary; Lord Lloyd, Colonies; Sir Andrew Duncan, Board of Trade; Mr. Herbert Morrison, Supply; Mr. Duff Cooper, Information; Mr. Ernest Bevin, Labour and National Service; Mr. L. S. Amery, India and Burma; Mr. Malcolm MacDonald, Health; Lord Woolton, Food; Viscount Caldicote, Dominions; Mr. Ernest Brown, Scotland; Lord Beaverbrook, Aircraft Production; Mr. H. Ramsbotham, Education; Mr. Robert Hudson, Agriculture; Sir John Reith, Transport; Mr. Ronald Cross, Shipping, and Mr. Hugh Dalton, Economic Warfare.

Mr. Chamberlain in a broadcast after his resignation of the Premiership:

Early this morning, without warning or excuse, Hitler added another to the horrible crimes which already disgrace his name by a sudden attack on Holland, Belgium and Luxembourg. In all history no other man has been responsible for such a hideous toll of human suffering and misery as he.

He has chosen a moment when perhaps it seemed to him that this country was entangled in the throes of a political crisis, and when he might find it divided against itself. If he has counted on our internal divisions to help him, he has miscalculated the minds of this people. . . .

The hour has come when we are to be put to the test, as the innocent people of Holland and Belgium and France are being tested already and you and I must rally behind our new leader, and with our united strength and with unshakable courage fight and work until this wild beast that has sprung out of his lair upon us is finally disarmed and overthrown.

OUR SKIPPER

We shall never Surrender

EVEN though large tracts of Europe and many old and famous states have fallen or may fall into the grip of the Gestapo, and all the odious apparatus of Nazi rule, we shall not flag or fail. We shall go on to the end; we shall fight . . . on the seas and oceans; we shall fight with growing confidence and growing strength in the air; we shall defend our island whatever the cost may be. We shall fight on the beaches; we shall fight on the landing grounds; we shall fight in the fields and in the streets; we shall fight in the hills. We shall never surrender.

Extract from Prime Minister's Speech of June 4, 1940.

There is a curious postscript to what is possibly the most famous speech in history. It is an established fact that Churchill actually delivered the speech himself, in the House of Commons. However, in 1979, the actor, Norman Shelley, claimed that, because the new Prime Minister was very busy and he was known for his impression of him, his voice was heard on the historic broadcast, later in the day, not Churchill's!

AIR RAID WARNINGS

Warning of impending air raids will be given by a fluctuating or "warbling" signal of varying pitch, or a succession of intermittent blasts sounded by hooters and sirens.

These signals may be supplemented by sharp blasts on police whistles.

The "RAIDERS PASSED" signal will be a continuous signal at a steady pitch.

IF POISON GAS has been used, warning will be given by HAND RATTLES. The ringing of HAND BELLS will announce that the danger from gas has passed.

Every householder, or head of a family or business, should learn now how to protect, in war-time, his own people and home from the effects of explosive bombs, incendiary bombs, and poison gas.

Sandbags, to protect against bomb blast, around the main entrance to the Law Courts, Corporation Street, c 1940.

SHIPS OF ALL SIZES DARE THE GERMAN GUNS

UNDER THE GUNS OF THE BRITISH FLEET, UNDER THE WINGS OF THE ROYAL AIR FORCE, A LARGE PROPORTION OF THE B.E.F. WHO FOR THREE DAYS HAD BEEN FIGHTING THEIR WAY BACK TO THE FLANDERS COAST, HAVE NOW BEEN BROUGHT SAFELY TO ENGLAND FROM DUNKIRK.

Belvedere Road, Erdington, 1940.

If the
INVADER
comes

WHAT TO DO — AND HOW TO DO IT

THE Germans threaten to invade Great Britain. If they do so they will be driven out by our Navy, our Army and our Air Force. Yet the ordinary men and women of the civilian population will also have their part to play. Hitler's invasions of Poland, Holland and Belgium were greatly helped by the fact that the civilian population was taken by surprise. They did not know what to do when the moment came. *You must not be taken by surprise.* This leaflet tells you what general line you should take. More detailed instructions will be given you when the danger comes nearer. Meanwhile, read these instructions carefully and be prepared to carry them out.

I

When Holland and Belgium were invaded, the civilian population fled from their homes. They crowded on the roads, in cars, in carts, on bicycles and on foot, and so helped the enemy by preventing their own armies from advancing against the invaders. You must not allow that to happen here. Your first rule, therefore, is :—

(1) IF THE GERMANS COME, BY PARACHUTE, AEROPLANE OR SHIP, YOU MUST REMAIN WHERE YOU ARE. THE ORDER IS "STAY PUT".

If the Commander in Chief decides that the place where you live must be evacuated, he will tell you when and how to leave. Until you receive such orders you must remain where you are. If you run away, you will be exposed to far greater danger because you will be machine-gunned from the air as were civilians in Holland and Belgium, and you will also block the roads by which our own armies will advance to turn the Germans out.

II

There is another method which the Germans adopt in their invasion. They make use of the civilian population in order to create confusion and panic. They spread false rumours and issue false instructions. In order to prevent this, you should obey the second rule, which is as follows :—

(2) DO NOT BELIEVE RUMOURS AND DO NOT SPREAD THEM. WHEN YOU RECEIVE AN ORDER, MAKE QUITE SURE THAT IT IS A TRUE ORDER AND NOT A FAKED ORDER. MOST OF YOU KNOW YOUR POLICEMEN AND YOUR A.R.P. WARDENS BY SIGHT, YOU CAN TRUST THEM. IF YOU KEEP YOUR HEADS, YOU CAN ALSO TELL WHETHER A MILITARY OFFICER IS REALLY BRITISH OR ONLY PRETENDING TO BE SO. IF IN DOUBT ASK THE POLICE-MAN OR THE A.R.P. WARDEN. USE YOUR COMMON SENSE.

Special Warnings To Workers

A scheme to give factory workers a special air-raid warning to avoid unnecessary interruption of production was discussed yesterday in London by the T.U.C.

The plan, drawn up by the Ministry of Home Security, Air Ministry, Unions and Employers' organisations, is based on a system of roof-watchers and look-out men who will give warnings only if it is really necessary.

BRITAIN SEIZES THE FRENCH FLEET
Ministry of Information Statement, July 4, 1940

It will be recalled that the French Government, relying upon the promises of Germany and Italy not to use her Fleet against France's former Ally, undertook by the terms of the armistice to allow their Fleet to pass into the hands of the enemy.

His Majesty's Government, having lost all faith in promises made by the Governments of Germany and Italy, felt that they were compelled, not only in their own interests, but also in the hope of restoring the independence and the integrity of the French Empire, to take steps to ensure that the French Fleet should not be used against them by the common enemy.

With this object in view steps were taken in the early morning of July 3 to place all French men-of-war in British ports under British control.

At the same time French vessels in ports of North Africa were offered certain conditions designed solely for the purpose of keeping them out of German hands.

It was explained to the officer in command that if none of these conditions were accepted Great Britain was prepared to take every step in order to ensure that none of these vessels should be used against her.

His Majesty's Government deeply regret that the French admiral in command at Oran refused to accept any of the conditions proposed, with the inevitable result that action had to be taken.

THE LORD MAYOR of Birmingham on Wednesday appealed for gifts binoculars for the use of the Army. His appeal was urgent as many binoculars were lost in the withdrawal of the B.E.F. from France. The Lord Mayor arranged to receive gifts at the Council House at noon yesterday and by half-past twelve thirty-seven pairs had been handed in. Later gifts raised the total to fifty.

More rifle drill for the Home Guard,
23rd September 1940.

The interior of The Empire Theatre,
Smallbrook Street/Hurst Street, October 1940.

The result of a direct hit on the Wesleyan and General Assurance Society, Steelhouse Lane, 26th October 1940.

Police investigate big factory fire

Police are investigating the cause of a fire which destroyed a Birmingham factory yesterday. The outbreak was discovered about an hour and a half after the employees had left.

Firemen were hampered by white-hot metal which spread in all directions. Several minor explosions threw clouds of sparks high in the air.

Woodbridge Road, Moseley, October 1940.

11

Petrol Up To 1s. 9¼d. Today

THE price of pool motor spirit is raised today by 1¼d. a gallon to 1s. 9¼d.—the highest price for 15 years—with the usual surcharges for North and West Scotland, etc. The Government has agreed to the increase, which follows an earlier rise of 2d. a gallon made on October 17.

FIFTY THOUSAND radio sets, now installed in motor-cars in Great Britain, will have to be dismantled soon and removed.

A new Emergency Powers (Defence) Regulation, issued by the Postmaster-General yesterday says: "No person shall use or have in his possession or under his control any radio receiving apparatus installed in any road vehicle."

The carrying of portable radio sets in cars is also forbidden. For the purposes of this regulation a radio set is deemed to be installed, even if it is not fixed in position, "in circumstances in which it can be readily adapted for use."

The exact date on which car radios must be dismantled is not fixed.

LEMONS are unobtainable in Birmingham. This is by no means surprising since Italy and Spain are the source of the supply.

"I haven't a lemon in the shop," confessed a fruiterer today, "and I don't give much for your chance of getting any. There may be a few during the next day or two, when a ship comes in, but the scarcity is certain to continue."

English apples may be had in a wide range, with Worcester Pearmains popular at 8d. to 10d. per lb. Imported apples are costing 10d. per lb. and cookers 3d. to 4d. Cultivated blackberries are available at 1s. per lb. Oranges are from 2s. to 3s. per dozen, according to size, and grapefruit 6d. each.

The roof of St Philip's Cathedral, 29th October 1940.

DEAR PROFITEER,— I do not write to you by name because I know how you detest publicity. You do like to hide your light behind a bushel, don't you?

Especially, shall I say, a bushel of onions.

Another reason for hiding your identity is because I do not know your name. You have a hundred names—as many, in fact, as the ways you have of turning a dishonest "pony."

What I want to say is this : Although the Government have power to stop profiteering, you still contrive to have a good run for my money.

You were in on the fruit racket back in the summer, weren't you? Then you cleaned up on dried peas and beans. You made a bit out of bricks, got in on the ground floor with onions, and are now busying about with the tinned tomatoes ramp.

Of course you know as much about bricks as you do about onions. Precisely nothing. But you could give the Artful Dodger a few tips on the science of picking pockets.

ALL ROUND ECONOMY

To make tea go much farther put a quarter of a pound of tea in the oven for ten or fifteen minutes or until well dry. Then put it between the folds of a newspaper and crush with a rolling-pin. You will be surprised to find how much further it goes.—J. Davison.

To save gas or other fuel when making a suet pudding, whether meat or fruit, cut a small piece of the suet paste about the size of a penny from the bottom of the paste. Then fill up the basin, and cover with a round of paste as usual, and the pudding will take much less time to cook, as the heat can get through the centre of the pudding immediately.—Mrs. B. N. Hughes.

Some people cannot wear Wellington boots because of the rubber being cold to their feet. A good way to avoid this is by making use of an old pair of fur-lined gauntlet gloves. Take out the fur and get a pair of socks the required size of the boot, then gum the skin side of the fur to the socks. These will be found most warm and comfortable.—Miss B. Rigby.

WORK OF THE HOUSE

When oiling wringers, if the bearings are lubricated with glycerine instead of ordinary oil, the clothes will not be marked should they come in contact with it.—Mrs. C. Phillpott.

Round the rim of cake-tins, etc., packed to the men of the Fighting Forces stick adhesive tape. It ensures the lid fitting tightly and keeps the contents airtight.—Mrs. S. John.

To prevent a draining-board rotting that is continually exposed to water make it waterproof in this way. Scrub the board well and allow it to dry, then rub it over with paraffin wax, forcing the wax into the wood by ironing your board with a warm iron.

E.N.S.A. PLANS MORE SHOWS

Plans to double concerts, sports and studies for the Services will be in operation by the autumn.

Six hundred jobless actors and actresses will help E.N.S.A. to give every soldier at least one show a fortnight.

Bigger libraries, lectures by schoolmasters and professors of first-class qualifications, optional lessons for all ranks, will, it is hoped, cater for every soldier.

Butter Ration Cut Two Ounces

The butter allowance is to be reduced from 6oz. to 4oz. from Monday next.

"This only affects people who have been in the habit of taking all their 6oz. ration in butter," a Food Ministry official said. "People who have normally drawn all their ration—6oz.—in margarine will not be affected."

17 DOWN

SEVENTEEN German aircraft were shot down in raids over this country yesterday. One of our fighters was lost.

Tindal Street School, Cromer Road, Balsall Heath, October 1940.

Holloway Head, October 1940.

The once-splendid dining room of the Great Western Hotel, at Snow Hill Station, November 1940.

GOVERNMENT EVACUATION SCHEME

The Government have ordered evacuation of registered school children.

If your children are registered, visit their assembly point at once and read the instructions on the notice board.

The name and address of the assembly point is given on the notice to parents.

Posters notifying arrival will be displayed at the schools at which the children assemble for evacuation.

Boarding school children who are usually given a half-term holiday so that they can get home will be disappointed this year. The Government, it was stated yesterday, hopes that schools will dispense with this holiday this year.

Evacuation time for pupils from St Chad's Roman Catholic School, Shadwell Street, at Snow Hill Station, c1940.

Queen Street/Highgate Road, 20th November 1940.

Moseley, November 1940.

From John Bright Street, looking towards New Street Station, 21st November 1940

The junction of Gooch Street and Bromsgrove Street, 21st November 1940.

Great Western Arcade, 25th November 1940.

The King visits Aston, 13th December 1940.

Carols, played by the Salvation Army Band, in the Minories (facing Bull Street), 24th December 1940.

Swanshurst Lane, Moseley, January 1941.

COAL hoarders may have their stocks seized : eggs —at last—are more plentiful : face powders and creams may soon be obtainable for a time : razor blades are to be still scarcer.

Such is to-day's News From the Home Front.

Alfred Road, Sparkhill, 2nd January 1941.

WOMEN WANTED

to take over the
BALLOON BARRAGE

The nightmare of Nazi airmen is Britain's balloon barrage. That's why it is one of the most important jobs in the country to keep those silver fish flying! And the WAAF have proved they can take over this important front-line job from the RAF!

It's a fine, healthy life for women who are fit and strong and fond of the open air. You must be 5' 1" or over, and aged between 17½ and 43. After a short training course, you will be posted to a balloon site. Sites are usually in or near a town. There you will live and work in a small community of about a dozen or so. When fully trained your minimum pay is 3/- a day *and all found*.

In addition to balloon operation, there are many other interesting trades open now in the WAAF. Every woman not doing vital work is asked to volunteer.

A Serviceman's wife does NOT lose her allowance on joining up, and she IS granted her leave to coincide with her husband's leave, subject only to urgent Service considerations.

Go to a Recruiting Centre* or Employment Exchange for fuller information. If you are in work, *they* will find out whether you can be spared from it. If you cannot go at once, send in the coupon.

WAAF

When this girl joined the WAAF six months ago, to become a balloon operator, she was badly under weight. Now she's back to normal. " You can tell them from me, it's a grand life!" she says.

*Single girls born between January 1st, 1918, and June 30th, 1922, come under the National Service Act and *must* go to the Employment Exchange, *not* a Recruiting Centre.

---

297 Oxford Street, London, W.1   3010   *AR 10*

Please send me full information about the trade of Balloon Operator in the WAAF.

Mrs.⎱
Miss⎰   *Cross out " Mrs." or " Miss "*

Address _____

County_____ Date of birth_____   *In confidence*

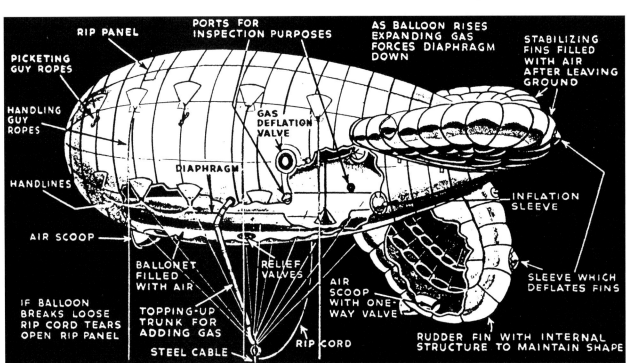

Showing the constructional details of a British barrage balloon. Fear of collision with the balloon or its trailing steel cable compels enemy bombers to fly high, where they are more vulnerable to our A.A. fire and less able to bomb with precision. The balloons cost about £100 each to construct. The gas for each filling costs about £25.

We could lose the war by Fire! Be ready for FIREBOMB FRITZ

The balloon barrage which effectively stops enemy dive bombers from approaching their targets, 1941.

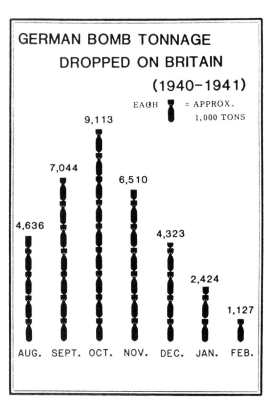

GERMAN BOMB TONNAGE DROPPED ON BRITAIN (1940–1941)

EACH = APPROX. 1,000 TONS

9,113
7,044
6,510
4,636
4,323
2,424
1,127

AUG. SEPT. OCT. NOV. DEC. JAN. FEB.

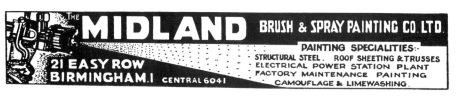

The Home Guard protect a German plane downed in Pype Hayes Park, 1941.

"Made in Germany, finished in England!" A wartime slogan that sums up the feeling at the time, 1941.

A new protective helmet for roof spotters, 1941. Unfortunately, it was made of asbestos!

Home Guard Parade marching down Colmore Row into Victoria Square, 23rd March 1941.

The premises of W.H. Smart & Co. Ltd., (ham and bacon curers), Birmingham Ham Market, Wrentham Street, 9th April 1941.

The Lord Mayor, Ald. Wilfrid Martineau, before acting as chairman at the re-opening of the Methodist Youth Club, with some of the guests, Perry Common Community Hall, 10th March 1941.

SHOP GIRLS, typists, dressmakers, usherettes —all girls, in fact, who have been thrown out of their normal employment by the war—are invited to sign on for war work at their local Labour Exchanges on Monday.

On this day the great drive begins to get 500,000 extra women into war industry. Officials will be ready with all the answers to the hundred and one questions the women will want to ask.

Who will look after my baby? How will I get to and from work? What will I be paid when trained? How do I live till then? Will you find me a job at the end of the training? And so on.

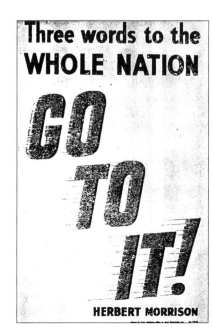

Nechells Green, 15th April 1941.

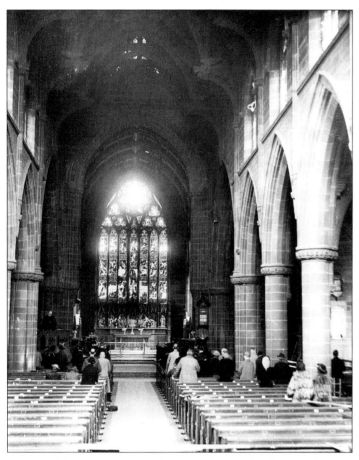

The Dinner Hour Service, conducted by Canon Guy
Rogers, St Martin's, 17th April 1941.

St. Martin's, 1941.

AERIAL BOMBARDMENT
Emergency Rest Centres

Persons whose houses have been destroyed or damaged by Enemy Action and who are
temporarily homeless may be accommodated in **REST CENTRES** until other
arrangements are made; similarly the **REST CENTRES** are available for
persons who have left their homes by reason of the proximity of Unexploded Bombs

CONVOY YOUR **COUNTRY** TO **VICTORY**
SAVE AND **LEND**
THROUGH OUR
NATIONAL SAVINGS GROUP

PICTURE FANS.

A for Anna Neagle who sings like a bird,
B for Boris Karloff who makes me feel scared,
C for Clark Gable who sends girls' hearts a-flutter,
D for David Niven who makes us all stutter.
E for Eleanor Powell who looks glamorous at nights,
F for Fred Astaire who dances in tights.
G for Gordon Harker whose voice sounds like thunder,
H for Hedy Lammar whose spell all men fall under.
I for Irene Dunn who makes love look exciting,
J for James Cagney who loves to be fighting.
K for Katherine Hepburn who's got a cute figure,
L for Lana Turner who's quite a gold digger.
M for Mickey Rooney who's always in trouble,
N for Ned Sparks who can knock back a double.
O for Oliver Hardy who's fair, fat and forty,
P for Pat Kirkwood who's inclined to be naughty.
Q for Queenie the dog we all fall for,
R for Robert Taylor the guy girls leave home for.
S for Spencer Tracy whose acting is terrific,
T for Tyrone Power who cruises the Pacific.
U for Una Merkel who acts quite the lady,
V for Victor Maclagan who'd look good in the Navy.
W for Will Hay (makes us think of D.C.S.),
X for (beats me, I'll leave you to guess).
Y for Yvonne who designs all the gowns
Z for Zeigfield Girls who banish men's frowns.

Brook Hill Road, Ward End, 28th April 1941.

Inside Information!

From the manufacture of Galvanised Hollow-ware to intricate 5-compartment Parachute Containers seems a radical departure. But to the staff of a Co-operative Wholesale Society's factory in the Midlands it presented no insuperable difficulties, for intelligence is the ability to adapt oneself to one's environment. They set to work with a will, and in a matter of months thousands of Parachute Containers and Inner Cells had been delivered to the Airborne Army which won undying fame on the Continent.

Yet another symbolic illustration of Co-operation in wartime.

Issued by the

CO-OPERATIVE WHOLESALE SOCIETY, LTD.

Edgbaston Street, showing Lease Lane (with the Market Hall at the top) and the Waggon & Horses (right), April 1941.

Addison Road, Nechells, 1941.

Newton Street, devastation after the night of 9th April 1941.

A job interview being conducted at a Birmingham Labour Exchange, 19th May 1941.

A female porter at New Street Station, 1941.

NATIONAL SERVICE (ARMED FORCES) ACTS

GRADE CARD.

Registration No. *BXX 22929*

Mr. *Percival T Lockwood*

whose address on his registration card is

21 Heath Green Rd B'ham.18.

was medically examined at **BIRMINGHAM MEDICAL BOARD (No.)**

on *2 0 MAY 1941*

and placed in

GRADE* ....

E.D. Until* ....(Medical Board stamp.)

Chairman of Board ....

Man's Signature *P T Lockwood*

*The roman numeral denoting the man's Grade (with number also spelt out) will be entered in RED ink by the Chairman himself, e.g., Grade I (one), Grade II (two) (a) (Vision). If the examination is deferred the Chairman will enter a date after the words "E.D. Until", and cross out "Grade"; alternatively, the words "E.D. Until............" will be struck out.

N.S. 55

Bankes Road, Small Heath, July 1941. Note the bedroom windows, on the left, have been blast-proofed.

M. A. LLOYD & SON Ltd.

DIRECTORS: L. A. LLOYD, E. C. LLOYD, H. L. LLOYD.

MANUFACTURERS OF

STATIONERS' SUNDRIES
AND
LADIES' HAND BAG FRAMES & FITTINGS
ALSO
ACCURATE PRESSED & MACHINED WORK

TELEGRAMS: "INKSTAND, BIRMINGHAM."
TELEPHONE: ASTON CROSS 1468

CONTRACTORS TO H.M. HOME AND COLONIAL GOVERNMENTS

PRINCIP ST., BIRMINGHAM, 4

21st May, 1941.

The Manager,
Ministry of Labour & National Service,
Employment Exchange,
281, Corporation Street,
BIRMINGHAM.

Dear Sir,

Re - Percival T. Lockwood,
21, Heath Green Road, B'ham.18.

You have our application for Registration under the Protected Establishments on account of the Ministry of Aircraft Production.

We have been busy for the last six months making tools and getting ready for production of the 20 m.m. Hispano Cartridge Link. We started production only two months ago, and are now turning out 30/40,000 a week.

Owing to the big change over, we have lost a lot of our labour during the last six months. Now the Ministry of Aircraft Production are pressing us to increase our output to 100,000 a week, so that you will see that we cannot part with the labour we have, as we find it exceedingly difficult to get any fresh work people.

Although Percy Lockwood is registered as a Cabinet Maker, we now use him as our maintenance hand, and are relying upon his services to help increase our production.

We are,
Yours faithfully,
for M. A. LLOYD & SON, LTD.

What should be your war-time nightcap?

FOR one reason or another, almost all of us have an extra strain to bear nowadays.

You may be working overtime: this imposes a physical and a nervous strain upon you. If, like so many people these days, you have also to endure emotional stress you have a further burden. And all of us have to armour ourselves against the general war "nerviness" that crops up now and then in the form of short-tempered irritability, or acute tiredness.

Our best defence is to have deep, healing sleep. Nothing is so restorative as a good night's sleep. Yet more than anything else — except actual air-raid conditions — it is this nervous tautness that prevents sleep, or, even when you "drop-off," keeps you uneasily on the surface of sleep. This is why, in war-time, your choice of a nightcap is especially important.

You will find that, after a cup of hot Horlicks last thing, you get the deep, sound sleep that is truly restoring. Unlike stimulants, which naturally tend to aggravate wakefulness, Horlicks has a soothing and quietening effect. In addition, Horlicks has the advantage of being highly nourishing, and so easy to digest that it puts no strain on the stomach during sleep. Horlicks is made from wheat, malted barley and pure full-cream milk — one of the best "protective" foods.

Let Horlicks help you to get good, truly restorative sleep *tonight*. Make it your regular nightcap, and see how it helps you stand the strain. For when you get the good sleep and the extra nourishment that Horlicks gives, you will be able to take both work and worry in your stride. Start tonight! Prices are the same as pre-war: from 2/-. Mixers from 6d. At chemists and grocers.

EMERGENCY STORE

The keeping qualities of Horlicks, combined with those already referred to, make it one of the most valuable of all foods for the emergency store cupboard. Even after it has been opened, Horlicks will keep in perfect condition if the screw-top is firmly replaced on the bottle. This is a great advantage, especially when you remember that Horlicks contains milk, is naturally sweet and is therefore very valuable in an emergency.

In order to ensure that a supply of Horlicks will always be available for people even in an emergency, depots have been established at 50 strategic points throughout the country. Large stocks of Horlicks are safely stored at these depots and will be drawn on whenever necessary.

HORLICKS

Millward Street, Bordesley, July 1941.

The Lord Mayor, Ald. Wilfrid Martineau (centre), takes part in a broadcast, 4th July 1941.

Millward Street, Bordesley, July 1941.

WHY AREN'T THERE *MORE* TRAINS ?

Factories turning out guns, bombers and fighters depend on the Railways for supplies.

To keep them working at top pressure the Railways must run thousands of additional goods trains by day and night.

The Railways must also keep the Nation's food, coal and export trades moving.

Essential trains must have first claim on the lines. *It is as vital to ration trains as it is to ration food.* The Railways are giving you every passenger train the tracks will take.

WE'LL BEAT HITLER BY HELPING ONE ANOTHER

BRITISH RAILWAYS

Handsworth Home Guard, with Frank Broom (the Aston Villa and England footballer), sitting second left, 1941.

Army manoeuvres in Pinfold Street, July 1941. This group was captured – fortunately it was not for real!

The mounted Home Guard awaits orders, Sutton Park, 7th July 1941.

Birmingham evacuees, hop-picking in Worcester during the school holidays, September 1941.

TAKE THEM BACK!
TAKE THEM BACK!
TAKE THEM BACK!

DON'T do it, Mother—

LEAVE THE CHILDREN WHERE THEY ARE

Due to the shortage of men, more women are needed in heavy industry, 1941.

A recruiting parade, outside the Council House, September 1941.

Carroty George

He's a great favourite in the kitchen, our Carroty George. He has a hundred and one ways of making himself agreeable. Given a chance he'll enter into your pots and pans with real relish. Even if you reduce him to dice he won't be cut up ; and he takes frying, steaming, stewing or boiling, in perfectly good part. He plays the leading part in

Club Carrots

Scrub and grate six large carrots and mix with a teaspoonful of finely shredded white heart of cabbage. Make a dressing of 1 small teacupful thick unflavoured custard, 1 tablespoon salad oil, 1 teaspoon vinegar, ½ teaspoon each mustard, pepper, and salt, and 1 tablespoon finely chopped pickles. Toast 4 thick slices of bread on each side, then slit open to make large pockets. Spread the insides of these pockets with margarine, and stuff with the filling. Serve at once. A first-rate supper dish.

WVS (Women's Voluntary Service) workers manage a field kitchen, part of one of the emergency food convoys rushed in to help in bombed areas, c 1941.

W·V·S CIVIL DEFENCE

HOW TO GET YOUR CARD FILLED IN.

All Courses are divided into four or multiples of four.

Four lessons in each subject will be given each week. (See Training Programme for details.) It is thus possible for you to take four lessons in any subject in one week. Alternatively, you can take lesson No. 1 on Monday one week, lesson No. 2 on Tuesday the following week, and so on.

After each lesson the Instructor will initial the appropriate square on your card.

At the end of the Course he will enter his comments in the "Remarks" column.

YOU **MUST** TAKE THESE SUBJECTS FIRST :
SQUAD DRILL
ARMS DRILL
ELEMENTARY MUSKETRY
ADVANCED MUSKETRY.

After that you may choose subjects in what order you wish.

● GO TO IT!

"D" COMPANY

21st Battalion Warwickshire (B'ham)

HOME GUARD

Name and Number KENDALL. J.S. 87/876

Rank VOL

Date of Issue 1 DECᵣ 1941

TO THE RECIPIENT

This is your Progress Card. Take a pride in it. Every initialled square is another step towards becoming an efficient Home Guard. You are a member of a Company that is proud of its men and its reputation. **You** can make us prouder still. **KEEP KEEN.** Turn up for your instruction regularly and make the heavy task of your Instructors worth while.

REMEMBER, ALL YOUR OFFICERS TAKE A PERSONAL INTEREST IN YOU GO TO THEM IF YOU ARE IN ANY DIFFICULTY.

See back of Card for Instructions.

When walking after dark to-night, For safety's sake wear something **WHITE**

For the pedestrian: Remember that when you can see the motorist the motorist probably can't see you. So wear or carry something white or luminous.

For the motorist: Remember you are in charge of a weapon that can kill. Be *careful* — be *considerate*.

★ THERE WERE 1,313 ROAD DEATHS IN DECEMBER—

The Lord Mayor, Ald. Norman Tiptaft, receives a presentation from Canada, 6th January 1942.

Ammunition box production, Austin Works, c 1942. This photograph was banned from use until the summer of 1945.

A Spitfire production line, Castle Bromwich
Aeroplane Factory, 1942.

K2 ambulance, made at the Austin Works, Longbridge, c 1942.

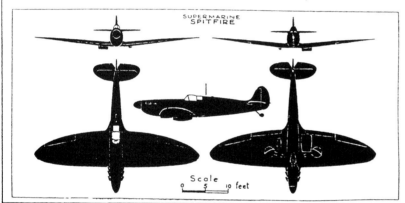

Single-seat fighter — *Great Britain*

THE SUPERMARINE SPITFIRE Mk I

THE Supermarine Spitfire single-seat fighter (1,030 h.p. Rolls-Royce Merlin II liquid-cooled motor and D.H. three-blade controllable-pitch airscrew). Low wing cantilever monoplane. Dark brown and green camouflage. Under surfaces: Starboard wing white, port wing black. All-metal construction with stressed metal covering. Eight Browning machine guns, four in each wing, fixed to fire forwards outside airscrew disc. Outwards retracting undercarriage. Fixed tail wheel. Radiator under starboard wing, oil cooler under port wing. Deep breasted nose, elliptical wings. Cantilever fin and rudder. Rounded tailplane.

Span 36 ft. 10 ins.; length 29 ft. 11 ins.; height 11 ft. 5 ins.; wing area 242 sq. ft.   Loaded weight 5,850 lb.
Max. speed 387 m.p.h. at 18,500 ft.   Duration 3·6 hours.   Initial climb 2,300 ft. per min.

SUPERMARINE SPITFIRE

Scale
0   5   10 feet

A lonely plane-spotter at work, c 1942.

A short break from working on aeroplane fuselages, Castle Bromwich Aeroplane
Factory, 1942.

31

WVS at work in a municipal park, 1942.

King Haakon of Norway (centre in dark coat) inspects a Guard of Honour, Colmore Row, 8th April 1942.

The King and Queen, as part of their endless journey around the British Isles, visit the children of Birchfield Road School, 25th April 1942.

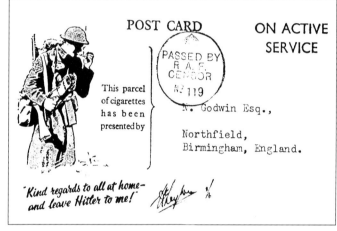

Members of the ATS (Auxiliary Territorial Service, later the WRAC) take a breather, c 1942.

The research team, led by Nobel Prize winner, Professor Sir Norman Haworth (centre), involved in pioneer work for The British Atomic Energy Project, University of Birmingham, c 1942.

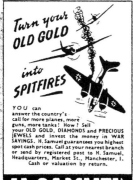
CHORUS girls of the touring revues are finding all billets taken by war workers in scores of the smaller manufacturing towns and are having to make shift in their dressing-rooms or among the theatre seats.

Many girls sing and dance with aching backs—the result of sleeping curled up on a "prop" basket.

Almost all the usual theatrical lodgings have been taken by munition workers, evacuees, or the military.

But for all the Alerts, blitzes, and comfortless nights, with perhaps a make-up box for a pillow, the girls carry on cheerfully.

Civil Defence volunteers, Bournbrook, c 1942.

Home Guard under-going anti-aircraft training with rocket projectors, 8th July 1942.

A new device for dealing with incendiary bombs in inaccessible corners, c 1942.

Sparkbrook fire-fighters ready to man the pumps and protect the shops in Stratford Road, c 1942.

Lucas ARP on the roof at Great King Street, Hockley, c 1942.

The Home Secretary, the Rt. Hon. Herbert Morrison (centre), meets fire-fighting chiefs, Central Fire Station, 13th September 1942.

A fire engine and trailer, 1942.

That's just my cup of tea!

The ration that gives more cups of better tea per pot.

LYONS TEA

J. LYONS & COMPANY LTD.

TRAIN TO WIN

APPLY TO THE EMPLOYMENT EXCHANGE
GOVERNMENT TRAINING SCHEMES
WITH PAID ALLOWANCES
100.
MINISTRY OF LABOUR AND NATIONAL SERVICE

A COMPLETE BIOGRAPHY OF
LORD HAW-HAW
OF ZEESEN
BY JONAH BARRINGTON AND FENWICK

COVER YOUR HAIR FOR SAFETY

YOUR RUSSIAN SISTER DOES!

Churchill

"I sometimes wonder whether people in this country sufficiently realise what Winston Churchill has meant, and continues to mean, not only to them but also to the Allied peoples, the United Nations, and to brave men and women everywhere in the world."—*Field-Marshal Smuts last night.*

He brought no gifts to cheer
  us when we met,
But blood and toil and toil and
  tears and sweat.
He could but point the path to
  Calvary
To Britons at the foot of
  Olivet.

*

When thunderous night en-
  gulfed uneasy day,
And iron Death went hurtling
  to the fray,
Through stern and scowling
  valleys of defeat
He held us, fighting, on the
  stubborn way.

He asked no comfort and he
  offered none,
Save what by hard endeavour
  might be won,
Nor toyed with easy dreams of
  after-days,
Nor rested while the task remained undone.

*

With every weapon of the
  hand and mind,
To bitter blows by wicked men
  resigned,
He fought. And at the vision
  of his blade
The tattered lackey limped and
  lagged behind.

*

When Norman arch lay prone
  with Gothic spire,
And Britain faced her long
  ordeal by fire,
He bade us seize upon the Nazi
  brand
And fling it back to light
  aggression's pyre.

There was no pose of Leader
  and the led.
To us, as Fury daubed the
  heavens red,
The highest to the humblest
  gave respect:
"The light of glory shines on
  all," he said.

This light he kindled, brothers
  of the flame,
Shall rid the shadowed lands
  of darkening shame,
And, in the peace of that
  undoubted day,
The light undying shine upon
  his name.

THURS. 15 OCT
WREN DAY

THE WOMEN'S ROYAL NAVAL SERVICE WANTS VOLUNTEERS
Your chance to learn all about the Service is NEXT THURSDAY

WREN DAY

On this day the W.R.N.S. travelling Interview Officer will be at

Six Ways, Aston, Birmingham.

If you are interested call between 10 a.m. and 5.30 p.m.

Applicants born in the period from January, 1918 to 30th June 1922 inclusive, must apply to their Local Employment Exchange.

WOMEN'S ROYAL NAVAL SERVICE

W.R.N.S.

Lord Dudley about to perform the opening ceremony at the exhibition of paintings from The Tate Gallery. Royal Society of Artists, New Street, 6th November 1942.

High Street, looking towards Dale End, c 1943.

...embers of the Fire Service, c 1943. It's often forgotten that ...great many women were involved in fire-fighting activities.

...ord Woolton, Minister for Food, visits a Birmingham Civic Restaurant, 26th February 1943.

HINT TO COMPANIES ON A "LONG-OVERDUE REFORM"

"ELECTRIFICATION of the Midland railway systems is long overdue," declared Ald. A. E. Ager, when referring to the problems of reconstruction in his address as chairman at the first annual meeting of the West Midlands Regional Council of the Labour Party, held in Birmingham yesterday.

FOD FACTS

APPLE HARVEST

Apples are plentiful, and it's grand to serve delicious apple sweets to the family. Eat all you can, revel in apple fool, apple tart, and apple dumpling; but think also of the Winter months ahead when fruit is unobtainable, and *for every pound of apples you eat now preserve another pound for future eating*. Winter meals will prove less of a problem if the larder is stocked with apple pulp, apple rings, apple and ginger jam, and apple chutney. Make the most of the apple harvest.

Apple Pulp

This is a quick and easy way of preserving apples. A large quantity of fruit can be stored in each jar and used later on for making into jam or for making apple puddings.

Peel and core the apples and remove any blemished parts. Stew in a saucepan with just enough water to prevent burning until the fruit is cooked through. While still boiling pour into *hot* bottles and seal immediately with hot lids. When using a screw-band give a half turn back to allow for expansion. Now immerse the bottles in a pan of hot water which must be raised to boiling point and boiled for five minutes. Take out the bottles to cool. Test next day. Remove screw-band or clip: if the seal is perfect it should be possible to lift the jar by the lid. If the lid comes off re-sterilise or use at once. For sweetened pulp follow the method given above, but add a little sugar to the fruit before it is brought to the boil.

Apple Rings

Here's a way of keeping apples that can be used for windfalls or blemished fruit.

Wipe the apples, remove the cores and peel thinly, cutting out any blemishes. Slice into rings about ¼ inch thick. Steep the rings for ten minutes in water containing 1½ oz. of salt to the gallon. Thread the rings on sticks or canes to fit across the oven or spread on trays. Dry very slowly until the rings feel like chamois leather. The temperature should not exceed 150° F. Turn once or twice during drying.

Swiss Apple

This is a quickly-made sweet which the children will love. *Ingredients :* 1 large apple, 1 heaped tablespoon rolled oats, 1 heaped teaspoonful sugar, 2 tablespoonfuls evaporated or top milk. *Quantity :* one helping. *Method :* Soak the rolled oats in the milk for an hour or more. Grate the unpeeled apple and add to the mixture with the sugar. Beat together.

THIS IS WEEK 4—THE LAST WEEK—OF RATION PERIOD No. 1

THE MINISTRY OF FOOD, LONDON, W.I.   FOOD FACTS No. 163

Gas-powered Midland Red Bus, Digbeth, 1943.

Because of the shortage of fuel some city buses were
converted to run on gas, produced by burning anthracite.
The trailer was then towed behind the bus, c 1943.

A NEW drive against careless
talk has been started by the
police and military with a threat
that licensed premises, clubs, and
hotels will be put out of bounds if
it is not checked.

In military and garrison towns
hotel and public-house proprietors
have been instructed to report to
the police any breach of the regulations. They have also been told
to inform their staffs that they must
report anything they overhear
while serving.

Honour Test for
Bus Passengers

Instead of a curfew at 9.15 p.m.
Birmingham buses will from February 21 run until 10 p.m.

After that time there will be
special buses for war workers, and
the general public will be put on
their honour not to ride in them.

A demolition man checks the steel hawser
needed to bring down an unsafe wall,
c 1943.

The 49th Bn. Royal Warwickshire Home Guard attack! 1943.

Exercises for the Home Guard, 1943.

NOBLE GIFT BY A BIRMINGHAM MAN

THE Lord Mayor of Birmingham (Councillor W. S. Lewis) announced last night that he had received a wonderful send-off in his effort to raise £60,000 for the R.A.F. Benevolent Fund during his year of office.

Mr. Douglas W. Turner, a well-known Birmingham business man and magistrate, has undertaken to pay £25,000 to the fund by seven yearly instalments

BOMBS on the Axis hour after hour . . . . 8,000-pounders on Pilsen, Essen, Berlin . . . . high-explosives coldly determined by Bomber Command to secure the maximum effect on Nazi armaments and supplies.

Bombs falling precisely and punctually, and, as photographs prove beyond question, hitting the target.

Among the boys who deliver them, twisting and weaving in their Bostons and Lancasters through the treacherous new fields of daisy-flak, there ride ace airmen from the Midlands.

They include 22-year-old veterans like **Erdington's Pilot Officer Bert Meagher**, thrice a visitor to Essen, his D.F.C. scored over Berlin, his D.F.M. won in a trip to Le Creusot

Dress for the Party . . .

We take off 18.50
after briefing.
It will be cold
in the turrets —
Plenty of clothes —
three pullovers,
roll top sweater,
four pairs socks —
Mother would laugh.
Of course I wear 'em
plus flying kit
gloves and scarf —
Now details —
revolver, torch,
pipe — baccy —
thermos, hot coffee,
money, clasp knife,
matches —
extra scarf and gloves!!!
Yes, mother —
I'll need 'em all . . . .
and then some!
chewing gum, chocolate
barley sugar, biscuits,
clean rag.

*   *   *
I worm myself
into the turret,
Helmet . . . . Parachute.
Plug in the Intercom.
Engines tested —
Captain asks '*All ready?*'
O.K.—
We're off
to another
Party.

*   *   *

You wouldn't think—would you?—that so many things were required to put one airman into the fight. Yet so it is—and with every fighting man the same. Thousands of details which must be made and paid for. If you realise this, you will see how much we must work, how much we must save. We cannot work and save too much. SAVE MORE.

. . . Wings for Victory

"The surest way," Matilda said,
"To give the Axis knocks
Is letting your
suspenders out
And wearing shorter socks.

The shorter sock saves
labour, dear.
And tons of precious wool —
Like General Alexander's
head,
It's practical and cool.

So do not search for
longer hose —
Forego those extra inches!
With shorter socks
make Hitler feel
Just where his own shoe
pinches!"

Wolsey

Stirling bomber production at the Austin Aero Works, c 1943.

RADIO PROGRAMMES

HOME SERVICE

3.0—Band of the East Yorkshire Regiment. 3.30—Evensong. 4.0—Griller String Quartet. 4.45—"Twice-told Tales." 5.0—Welsh programme. 5.30—Children's Hour.
6.0—News; announcements. 6.30—"Mr. Cropper Looks at Life" (No. 6). 6.45—Battersea Grammar School Boys' Band and the Norwich Lads' Club Band. 7.15—Scottish Half-hour. 7.45 — "Youth Must Have Its Swing," with Sid Field and George Black's Youngsters. 8.15—Brains Trust.
9.0—News. 9.25—"British Craftsmen." 9.50 — "Love Behind the Lattice," by Edward Knoblock. 10.20 "My Faith and My Job": Talk. 10.35—Dostoevsky and Turgenev: A study by V. S. Pritchett. 11.15—Philharmonic Harp Trio. 11.35—Victor Silvester's Ballroom Orchestra. 12.0—News.

FOR THE FORCES

3.0—Home. 3.30—The Bob Crosby and Casa Loma Orchestra. 4.0—Felton Rapley (organ). 4.20—Maurice Kasket's Orchestra and Edmundo Ros's Rumba Band. 5.0—B.B.C. Revue Chorus and Orchestra. 5.30—"The Trojans": Berlioz's last opera on records.
6.0—Home. 6.30 — Australian news. 6.40—New Zealand news. 6.50—South African news. 7.0—American Sports news. 7.5—"These You Have Loved": Records. 7.50—B.B.C. Midland Light Orchestra. 8.25—Jack Payne's Orchestra.
9.0—Home. 9.25—"Into Battle." 9.35—"The Music Society of Lower Basin Street" (No. 11). 10.0—"Tuesday Radiogram." 10.30—Harold Collins' Orchestra (recording).

St John the Baptist Church,
Chapel House Street/Deritend,
c 1943.

PARENTS' PETITION

ACCOMMODATION AT STECHFORD ROAD

THREAT TO KEEP CHILDREN AWAY

At a recent meeting of the Birmingham Education Committee a petition was submitted on behalf of the parents of children attending the Stechford Road School and living on the Firs Estate and the Ideal Homes Estate, Castle Bromwich.

They asked the Education Committee to take over from the Public Health Department the existing day nursery at the corner of the Heathway, transfer the children to another day nursery about 200 yards away, then use the first day nursery as an infants' school to relieve Stechford Road School and, meanwhile, erect a temporary infants' school on or near the Firs Estate before next winter.

The petitioners say that if the suggestions are not complied with it is feared there will be serious trouble next winter, as most of the petitioners are not prepared to send their children to school in bad weather.

"MORE AND BETTER BATHS"

"We are becoming swimming-minded," said Mr. H. A. Cole, Secretary of the Central Council of Recreative Physical Training, when he advocated "more and better baths" at a meeting of the Royal Life-Saving Society in Birmingham yesterday.

He called for more instruction in swimming and life-saving for schoolchildren as a means to a healthier post-war nation.

MORE ORANGES FOR MIDLANDS

A further supply of oranges has been received in the West Midlands, sufficient for a further 1lb to be drawn by every holder of a child's ration book (R.B.2)

Retailers will receive sufficient oranges for this purpose for a period of five days after receiving their supplies. Wholesalers have been authorised to release supplies to retailers to-morrow.

NOT SUITABLE FOR FAMILY LIFE

Flats are condemned as unsuitable for personal and family life, in a report, published to-day, of the evidence of the Town and Country Planning Association before the Ministry of Health's advisory committee on housing for the under £5 a week family.

"Your neighbour's wireless and piano, his loud voice and parties up to 1 o'clock in the morning, not to speak of his quarrels, are intolerable," says the report. "So is the continual feeling of restraint involved in taking care yourself not to disturb your neighbour.

"Anyone who has experience in the management of property will acknowledge that quarrels between neighbours are many times more frequent in blocks of flats than on cottage estates."

The report regards the nursery school to which flat children go as a "terrible commentary on the bankruptcy of our present way of life," and urges that a national code of housing standards should be framed for the under £5 a week family (pre-war figure).

The houses should be suitable for families of five, with outlook, privacy, and the placing of larder and kitchen carefully weighed and balanced, rows of semi-detached houses being varied by terraces of up to 10 or 12 houses.

"BROWNS" DAY

SMOOTHER WORKING IN BIRMINGHAM

Mr. and Mrs. Brown, of Birmingham, came to town to-day to get their new ration books and identity cards—and so did a lot of other people in the city whose names begin with BR, for this was the day allotted to them solely.

They all had a pleasant surprise, particularly the Browns. At no time did the two queues exceed more than 400 or 500 at one time. Strangely enough the line of waiting people including the Browns moved faster than the others.

At the head of the queues this morning sat a young girl with an automating adding machine. As each person passed by he or she was asked to call out how many cards and books were being applied for. It was all quite simple. By 10 a.m. the official recording read 2,800, and up to 11 a.m. it was 4,865. At 12.30 p.m. the figure was 7,300. Not all these people had been dealt with by this time, but they had at least got inside the Civic Centre, and once inside it was only a matter of a few minutes before they are out again.

GUERRILLA FIGHTER

No uniform, no medals for her. But she's tough. She fights with her wits, her energy, her belief in England—in YOU. She's fighting now in the streets, knocking at your door asking you to join the battle by putting your back into saving. Give her a hand. Put every shilling you can into National Savings Certificates—either through your Savings Group, the Post Office Savings Banks, or the Birmingham Municipal Bank. Savings Certificates cost 15/-, and you can also buy them by instalments with 6d., 2/6 and 5/- Savings Stamps. *Get into the fight !*

BUY SAVINGS CERTIFICATES

" By the way, the wife's gone to Switzerland—any objection to me joining her later ? "

BIRMINGHAM HOME GUARD

Signalling Certificate

This is to Certify that
(Rank) PTE (Name) KENDALL
(Batt.) 21st WARWICK H.G.
has passed a signalling test in accordance with the requirements as laid down in Home Guard Instruction No. 25 (Signalling) 1941, and has qualified as a 1st. Class SIGNALLER with the following results:-

BUZZER- at the rate of 6 words per minute ..98..%
LAMP - ,, ,, 4 ,, ,, 98 %
FLAG - ,, ,, 4 ,, ,, 100 %
PROCEDURE ... ... P..%
WRITTEN EXAMINATION ... .P....%

Major

Zone Communications Officer
for Colonel, Zone Commander

Birmingham Zone H.Q. Date 22 July 43.

B Co. 41st Warks. (B'ham) Bn. Home Guard Officers, 1943/4.

Meat — the fighter's mainstay

Well-fed, well-trained fighters have the split-second response needed in the terrific pace of modern warfare. And meat is one of the finest energizing foods. Armour's Canned Meats include Luncheon Meat, Chopped Ham, Pork Sausage Meat, Ox Tongues, Lunch Tongues, "Treet" and Corned Beef — these products are helping our fighting men and, in limited quantities, provisioning the civilian population.

Armour
MEAT & MEAT PRODUCTS
Food producers since 1867

ARMOUR & COMPANY LIMITED, London and Birmingham.

Lucas employees present a mobile canteen to the YMCA, for use with the Armed Forces, Great Hampton Street, c 1943.

"CIVVIES" FOR SOLDIERS

Relatives have to give up coupons

Many soldiers wives, mothers, and sisters are complaining that they have to part with their personal clothes coupons to "buy" "civvies" for their men on leave.

Non-commissioned soldiers, sailors, and airmen do not have coupons of their own.

Because officers experienced the same difficulty an arrangement was made to enable them to use 21 of their personal kitting-out coupons every year to buy civilian sports clothes.

The War Office considers that "other ranks" should have sufficient civilian clothes left from pre-service days to wear during leaves. The reply from the men —particularly the younger age groups—is that they have outgrown their "civvies."

BIRMINGHAM HIPPODROME

5.10

TWICE NIGHTLY
MONDAY, SEPT. 20th, 1943

7.25

Telephone : MIDland 2576-77

Proprietors	... ...	THE HAYMARKET CAPITOL LTD.
Joint	} ...	{ MARK OSTRER and
Managing Directors		{ L. W. FARROW
Direction	... ...	GEORGE BLACK
Licensee and Manager	...	BERTIE ADAMS
Press Representative	...	LAWSON E. TROUT, F.Inst.P.
Musical Director	... ...	SYDNEY CORNESS
(THE GENERAL THEATRE CORPORATION LTD.)		

In accordance with the requirements of the Licensing
Justices:—
(a) The public may leave at the end of the performance by all
exits and entrances other than those used as queue waiting rooms
and the doors at such exits and entrances shall at the time be open.
(b) All gangways, passages and staircases shall be kept entirely free
from chairs or any other obstruction. (c) Persons shall not be
permitted to stand or sit in any of the intersecting gangways. If
standing be permitted at the rear of the seating sufficient space
shall be left for persons to pass easily to and fro. (d) The fireproof
curtain shall at all times be maintained in working order and shall
be lowered at the beginning of and during the time of every
performance.

"Alert" and "All Clear" signals will be advised to
patrons by means of illuminated signs which are placed
at each side of the stage. Those desiring to leave may
do so, but the performance will continue.

PRICES OF ADMISSION
(Including Entertainments Tax)
Boxes 22/- and 16/6, Imperial Fauteuils 5/-, Fauteuils 4/-,
Stalls 3/-, Grand Circle 4/6, Circle 3/-, Balcony 9d.

LEW & LESLIE GRADE invite you to

"LAUGH AND BE HAPPY"

1 OVERTURE

2 LAUGH AND BE HAPPY with
   the Entire Company

3 MARIETTA DANCERS

4 ANCASTER
   Unique !

5 HAL MONTY
   introduces himself
   and introduces—

6 NAN KENWAY &
              DOUGLAS YOUNG
   Stars of Radio's Famous Feature
   " Howdy Folks "
   Very Tasty—Very Sweet

7 MILITARILY YOURS
   Eve Clare and the
              Marietta Dancers

8 HAL MONTY
   What a Life !

9 INTERVAL
   SYDNEY CORNESS and his ORCHESTRA

10 MARIETTA DANCERS

11 "MEET MR. BROWN"
   Nan Kenway & Douglas Young,
   Hal Monty & Eve Clare

12 BROADWAY BOYS
                  & BRENDA
   The Limit in Eccentricity

13 NAN KENWAY &
              DOUGLAS YOUNG

14 HAL MONTY
   Laugh and Be Happy

15 MARIETTA DANCERS
   introducing NAN KENWAY

16 "THE ART OF DISROBING"
   as shown by EVE CLARE

17 HARRY LESTER and his
                  HAYSEEDS
   with Rufus, Gufus and Grand-
   pappy
   Your Country Cousins come to
   Town

18 FINALE
   The Entire Company

Manager	... ...	William Gill
Stage Manager	...	Ted Hayes
Musical Director	...	James Peverley
Production	...	Albert J. Knight

(For Lew & Leslie Grade)

F Company, British Pens Home Guard, Bearwood Road, 1943.

IMPERIAL CHEMICAL INDUSTRIES LIMITED

LONG SERVICE CERTIFICATE

Presented to

Edward Broadbent

with the Good Wishes of the
Chairman and Directors
in appreciation of

Forty Years Service

completed on

1st December, 1943

Chairman

ICI

CITY OF BIRMINGHAM

EMERGENCY POWERS (DEFENCE)

FIRE GUARD.

B/469

Certificate

For the purposes of Article 11 (1) *(a)* and the Second Schedule, Part II (8) of the Fire Guard (Business and Government Premises) Order, 1943.

This is to certify that

Mr. Thomas Henry Yearsley

of 18 Witherford Way, Birmingham, 29,

has been appointed a   Fire Guard

Street Fire Party Leader

in the area of the Local Authority and is thereby exempted from duties pursuant to the Fire Guard (Business and Government Premises) Order, 1943, except duties during his working hours under arrangements in force for any non-residential premises.

Dated this 22nd day of November 1943.

Authorised Officer for and on behalf of the Local Authority.

This certificate is the property of the Local Authority, and must be surrendered on the cessation of the said duties.

P35982 B2 (a) 1339/16

CHINESE MISSION AT BOURNVILLE.

FOUR members of the Chinese Mission who have been touring this country paid a visit to Bournville on December 17th. They were received by Dame Elizabeth Cadbury, Chairman of the Bournville Village Trust, and by Mr. Paul Cadbury on behalf of the Firm. They made a short tour of the Estate and called at the Continuation School, where a Christmas party was in progress, and at the Works saw something of the Cocoa Block. After tea, Mr. Paul Cadbury spoke on the research work in housing and town planning which is being financed by the Village Trust and that which is being carried out by the West Midlands Group on Post-war Reconstruction and Planning, particularly as regards the distribution of industry. The guests asked many pertinent questions and touched also on a number of points of industrial administration. The visit was under the auspices of the Ministry of Information.

1944

WHEN a soldier returns to this country from overseas and marries an officer or member of the ATS to whom he had been engaged, she is to be granted the same amount of leave as married ATS whose husbands have returned.

Such ATS can claim:—

Husband returned for a limited period after an absence of over one year, maximum fifty-six days (twenty-eight days paid, twenty-eight days unpaid).

Husband returned on sixty-one days' leave instead of returning on the Python scheme, twenty-eight days paid, remainder to be covered by relegation to the unemployed list.

Husband returned on thirty days' leave in lieu of Python from BLA, thirty days paid.

Husband returned on Python scheme; paid leave for the same period as his disembarkation leave.

Husband returned prisoner of war; forty-two days paid leave

WHAT will Hitler do now that grim fate is overtaking him and all his dreams of political grandeur and military glory are evaporating?

Will he fight on, or will he flee for his life?

Will he end his life in some spectacular way, as those who have known him long enough have always suspected he might if things went wrong, or will he give himself up to the Allies in a spirit of self-immolation, to die dramatically for the cause of Nazism in the belief that in his way he can best perpetuate his cruel creed?

He has always boasted about his strong nerves and urged those around him to keep cool heads. Strong nerves have always been one of his favourite themes, which is something probably not very unusual in a masochist.

"One People, one Reich, one Leader!"

Henry Street/Heneage Street, Aston, 1944.

B.C.S. Ltd.
Card 40.

BIRMINGHAM
CO-OPERATIVE SOCIETY, LTD.

Registered Office : HIGH STREET, BIRMINGHAM.

Member's No. *38161*

Name *Grace Mary Lockwood*

INSTRUCTIONS.

1.—Always remember that the above is the number of your Pass Book.

2.—After making a purchase tell the shopman your number and get from him a paper Check bearing that number, and the amount of your purchase.

3.—Always put your Share number on every order for goods.

4.—Remember that if a member gives, or a shopman writes a wrong number, the dividend on that purchase will be drawn by the wrong person.

5.—Members are particularly desired to file each check and compare the amount of their purchases quarterly.

6.—Keep the checks until the voucher has been received with the amount of purchases credited, and, if incorrect, apply to office.

7.—Bring your Pass Book during the third week of quarter, and leave at the office or store.

This card is necessary to obtain admission to Quarterly or Mid-quarterly Meetings and/or for the purpose of voting at the Registered Office of the Society for the election of President, Auditor, General Committee, and Educational Committee.

RECORD OF VOTING AT HIGH STREET PREMISES.

		SEP 1943	MAR 1944

THE BIRMINGHAM PRINTERS, LIMITED, 42, HILL STREET

LONDON COLLEGE OF MUSIC
FOUNDED 1887   INCORPORATED
GREAT MARLBOROUGH STREET, LONDON, W.1.

EXAMINATION IN THEORETICAL MUSIC

BIRMINGHAM Centre

Audrey Hill

is requested to attend for Examination at

IMPERIAL HOTEL, TEMPLE STREET
BIRMINGHAM

WEDNESDAY 1   APL 1944

on

at *9.30* o'clock precisely.

Candidate's Official No. *1297795*

(This number must be quoted in all correspondence.)

Subject :—THEORY OF MUSIC

Section :— *Primary*

¶ The Candidate MUST BRING THIS PAPER ON THE DAY OF EXAMINATION, and deliver the same to the Supervisor on entering the Examination Room. The Paper will be returned in due course with the Examiner's award.

South African Premier, General Smuts, receives the Freedom of the City from the Lord Mayor, Ald. Lionel Alldridge, Town Hall, 19th May 1944.

WHEN you are feeling run down, go to the nearest hospital.

Spend a morning playing games in the open, do a course of physical exercises, or perhaps some handicraft. Have a midday meal at the hospital and attend a lecture or a "Brains Trust" in the afternoon. Rest a while and go home in the evening "rehabilitated."

That is the prospect which Mr. Willink, Minister of Health, has opened to every man, woman, and child in this country.

As part of the continuing war effort, local girls take on the unusual job (for that time) of forming a barge crew, Tyseley Wharf, 27th May 1944.

CHANCELLOR OF EXCHEQUER,
Treasury Chambers,
Great George Street,
S.W.1.
5th June, 1944.

Dear Sir,

The Chancellor of the Exchequer is very grateful to your Company for lending the further sum of £25,000 to the country free of interest, making up the amount lent in this way to £55,000.

Sir John Anderson would be glad if you would convey to the Directors his warm appreciation of the spirit which prompts this help in the War effort.

A certificate will be sent to you shortly giving title to repayment of the further loan.

Yours faithfully,

N. Tucker.

The Secretary,
Messrs. Jarrett, Rainsford & Laughton Ltd.

BSA, Small Heath, c 1944.

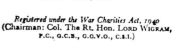

249th Week of War

DEDICATION

In this hour not only the armed forces battling across the waters but the whole nation is under test. Believing that God is using us to fulfil His high purpose, the King last night broadcast, in words which lift up the heart, a call to his people to dedicate themselves anew in the crusading spirit of the dark days of 1940. This is the message which his Majesty sends:

"Four years ago our Nation and Empire stood alone against an overwhelming enemy, with our backs to the wall. Tested as never before in our history, in God's providence we survived that test; the spirit of the people, resolute, dedicated, burned like a bright flame, lit surely from those Unseen Fires which nothing can quench.

MORE NEWS ABOUT JAP CAPTIVES

The Government has published a 16-page handbook giving information about prisoners of war in the Far East. Next of kin will be given free copies soon.

This is the first step taken by the new Government Bureau which Mr. Anthony Eden told Parliament yesterday now exists to deal with inquiries from relatives of Far East prisoners.

SIRENS TEST TO-MORROW

There will be a full test of all air raid warning sirens in the West Midlands at noon to-morrow. The test will comprise: "Raiders passed" signal for one minute; short interval; "alert" signal for one minute; short interval; "raiders passed" signal for one minute.

The test will not take place if actual "alert" conditions exist at noon or have occurred between Tuesday midnight and noon.

QUIET tip to women from the National Hairdressers' Federation—Don't have a cold permanent wave till well after the war—it's dangerous.

Not because the system is bad in itself. America has taken up the idea and many of the most famous stores advertise "Cold Perms" for sale at about 10s. a packet for home use.

The trouble is, according to the National Executive of the N.H.F., that the right chemicals are being put to much more serious use just now, and are not on the market for beauty purposes.

Workers from Coventry Road Garage, c 1944.

ALLIED ARMIES BEGAN THE LIBERATION OF EUROPE EARLY YESTERDAY MORNING WHEN THE GREATEST INVASION OF ALL TIME WAS LAUNCHED WITH LANDINGS FROM SEA AND AIR AT SEVERAL POINTS ON THE COAST OF NORMANDY. LATE LAST NIGHT FIGHTING WAS GOING ON IN THE STREETS OF CAEN, AN IMPORTANT ROAD JUNCTION 10 MILES INLAND AT THE BASE OF THE CHERBOURG PENINSULA.

White Hart, Bracebridge Street/Aston Road, 1944.

55

F5 Sector Staff Officers, 1944.

In the years when our Country

was in mortal danger

L/CPL DICKERS A.R.

who served May 1940 to 31st December 1944.

gave generously of his time and

powers to make himself ready

for her defence by force of arms

and with his life if need be.

George R.I.

THE HOME GUARD

Let's make it
another great
Savings year!
We've got to
keep on saving
to help win
the war...
and for the tasks
which lie ahead

Parties to — Lest we forget — Wounded

Under the Auspices of the

Alexandra Musical Society.

The wounded Sailors, Soldiers, Airmen, and Merchantmen who attended the party given by

Birmingham District Co-Operative Guild

on *Feb 23rd 1945* at *Co-Operative Cafe*

wish to convey their grateful thanks for the kind hospitality extended to them.

The party was much enjoyed by all.

ERNEST C. THOMAS, Hon. Organising Secretary,
Alexandra Musical Society, 249, Albert Road, Aston, Birmingham, 6.

The girls of Jarrett, Rainsford and Laughton, Alvechurch Road, West Heath, 1945.

CASUALTY lists in this war, 1939-1945, cannot yet be listed finally, obviously. But these are figures given by Mr. Churchill in April:

1939—1945

	Killed	Missing	Wounded	Prisoners	Totals
U. Kingdom ..	216,287	30,967	255,142	183,242	685,638
Canada	31,439	4,163	45,251	8,367	89,220
Australia	19,430	6,955	35,595	25,276	87,256
N. Zealand ..	9,334	934	17,978	8,501	36,747
S. Africa	6,030	512	12,632	14,629	33,803
Colonies	5,044	14,014	4,840	6,754	30,652
India	19,420	13,327	51,038	79,701	163,486
Totals	306,984	70,872	422,476	326,470	1,126,802

1914—1918

For the first World War, 1914 to 1918, the Empire casualties were:

	Deaths	Wounded
Gt. Britain & Ireland	812,317	1,849,494
Canada ..	62,817	166,105
Australia	60,456	154,722
N. Zealand	18,212	45,946
S. Africa..	9,032	17,843
Colonies ..	53,653	82,163
India	73,432	84,715
Totals	1,089,919	2,400,988

RAIDS.—Blitz, buzz bomb and V-bomb killed 59,793 and injured 84,749 so much that they had to be treated in hospital—a total of 144,542.

MERCHANT NAVY. — The Germans intensified the U-boat war this time, and 30,179 Merchant Navy men are known to have been killed or are missing.

ADOLF HITLER is dead. Grand Admiral Doenitz, Commander-in-Chief of the German Navy, has been appointed the new Führer. The German radio gave the news to the world at 10.25 last night in the following words: 'It is reported from the Führer's headquarters that our Führer, Adolf Hitler, has fallen this afternoon in his command post in the Reich Chancellery, fighting to his last breath against Bolshevism.

Victory flags on top of the Co-op building, High Street, 7th May 1945.

Scale of War Gratuity

Royal Navy	Army	Royal Air Force	Monthly rate of gratuity
Ratings and Other Ranks			
Ordinary Seaman Able Seaman	Private Lance-Corporal	A.C.II A.C.I L.A.C.	**10/-**
Leading Seaman	Corporal Lance-Sergeant	Corporal	**12/-**
Petty Officer	Sergeant	Sergeant	**14/-**
Chief Petty Officer	Staff-Sergeant	Flight Sergeant	**16/-**
—	Warrant Officer II	—	**18/-**
—	Warrant Officer I	Warrant Officer	**20/-**
Officers			
Midshipman Acting Sub-Lieut.	Second Lieutenant	Acting Pilot Officer Pilot Officer	**25/-**
Warrant Officer Sub-Lieut.	Lieutenant	Flying Officer	**30/-**
Commissioned Warrant Officer	—	—	**32/6**
Lieutenant	Captain	Flight Lieutenant	**35/-**
Lieut.-Commander	Major	Squadron Leader	**40/-**
Commander	Lieut.-Colonel	Wing Commander	**45/-**
Captain	Colonel	Group Captain	**50/-**
Commodore 1st or 2nd Class	Brigadier	Air Commodore	**55/-**
Rear Admiral	Major General	Air Vice-Marshal	**60/-**
Vice Admiral	Lieut.-General	Air Marshal	**65/-**
Admiral	General	Air Chief Marshal	**70/-**
Admiral of the Fleet	Field Marshal	Marshal of the R.A.F.	**75/-**

Note : The above War Gratuities are not payable to certain categories of personnel who are not on Service rates of pay.

The war in the West is over. Full, unconditional surrender to the Western Allies and to Russia was made by the Germans at Gen. Eisenhower's headquarters at Rheims, at 2.41 a.m. French time to-day. Jodl, Wehrmacht Chief of Staff, signed for the Germans.

An American soldier reads the Evening Despatch and the news of VE Day, 8th May 1945.

Mr. Churchill made the eagerly-awaited official announcement of the end of the war in Europe in a VE-Day broadcast to the nation this afternoon.

Hostilities will formally cease at one minute after midnight to-night, but in order to save lives the " cease fire " was actually sounded yesterday, he said.

VICTORY

VE party in Lingard Street, Nechells.

LORD MAYOR'S MESSAGE

"I AM PROUD OF BIRMINGHAM"

The Lord Mayor's Parlour,
The Council House,
Birmingham 1.

VE-DAY.

The great moment is here. The swift, significant events of recent days detract nothing from its greatness, from our profound sense of relief, nor from our proud recognition of the gallantry of every fighting man in the British Navy, Army and Air Force and in the fighting Services of our gallant Allies.

I say with all reverence and rejoicing " Thank God."

On this day of days let each one of us give thanks either at our usual or nearest place of worship, or in our own home, or at our work.

To-morrow at 11 a.m. at the Hall of Memory we hold a general Service of Thanksgiving—no one of any religious denomination or belief is excluded.

Yes, I am proud of Birmingham and its citizens. The City has known many dark and anxious days and thousands have lost their loved ones—we think of them very specially at this moment. Thousands of us still have our loved ones away, many still in danger or as prisoners of war. May God grant us true understanding of this His supreme gift—the gift of Freedom. I hope we can keep the clear knowledge of it throughout our lives and, to our little utmost, help build that better world which can be made given less selfishness on all our parts.

We will do well to heed the recent words of our Prime Minister and rejoice soberly, conscious of the great task still ahead. The citizens of a city which, in its workshops, offices and services, has played so great a part in the achievement of this long-sought Victory, need no call from me to celebrate that Victory thankfully, cheerfully and worthily.

W. T. WIGGINS-DAVIES,
Lord Mayor.

VE Day celebrations by Galloways Corner, New Street, 8th May 1945.

VE Day, New Street.

100,000 British Troops in Germany Go Gay

TOASTS TO THE FALLEN, AND TO LASTING PEACE

VE-Day was celebrated by over 100,000 British troops in Germany with bonfires, Verey lights of a dozen colours, and festivities in every mess and billet from the Weser to the Rhine, from the Rhine to the Elbe, and from the Baltic to Brussels.

During the Victory Parade, the Lord Mayor, W.T. Wiggins-Davies, meets members of the McGeoch Works Fire Brigade, 13th May 1945.

BIRMINGHAM CITY TRANSPORT.

VICTORY CELEBRATIONS, 1945.

THE

ILLUMINATED TRAMCAR AND OMNIBUS

WILL RUN TO-MORROW (SATURDAY), MAY 12th, 1945, AS UNDER:—

ILLUMINATED TRAMCAR.

Leave Kyotts Lake Road (8.20 p.m.) for Martineu Street (8.35 p.m.) to Perry Barr terminus (9.0 p.m.) via Six Ways, Aston to Villa Road terminus (9.20 p.m.) via Lozells Road to Victoria Road —Park-road junction (9.30 p.m.) to Witton terminus (9.45 p.m.) via Six Ways to Dale End (10.0 p.m.) to Kyotts Lake Road.

ILLUMINATED OMNIBUS.

Leave Kyotts Lake Road (7.20 p.m.) via Shaftmoor Lane for Nailstone Crescent (7.45 p.m.) via No. 32 bus route to Hall Green terminus (7.55 p.m.) via Baldwins Lane to Baldwins Lane terminus (8.0 p.m.) to Springfield Road—College Road junction (8.12 p.m.) via No. 1 bus route to Moseley Village (8.20 p.m.) to Maypole terminus (8.35 p.m.) via Maypole Lane to Warstock terminus (8.42 p.m.) via Yardley Wood Road to Yardley Wood (Priory Road) terminus (8.54 p.m.) via No. 13a bus route to Colmore Row (9.24 p.m.) to Moseley Village (9.44 p.m.) to Kyotts Lake Road via Moseley Road.

IN CASE OF INCLEMENT WEATHER THE VEHICLES WILL NOT RUN.

Council House, Birmingham.

∼∼∼The Price of Victory∼∼∼

TOTAL casualties suffered during the war by the Armed Forces, Auxiliary Services and the civilian population of the U.K. were 950,794. Of these 357,116 were killed ; 369,267 wounded ; 178,332 prisoners of war or internees ; 46,079 missing. Those killed in the Services were— Royal Navy, 50,758 ; Army, 144,079 ; R.A.F., 69,606. Navy wounded, 14,663 ; Army 239,575 ; R.A.F., 22,839. Civilians killed, 60,595 ; wounded, 86,182 ; Merchant Navy and Fishing Fleets, killed, 30,248 ; wounded, 4,707 ; Women's Services, killed, 624 ; wounded, 744 ; Home Guard, killed, 1,206 ; wounded, 557.

No big rush for basic petrol in Birmingham on first day of issue

IT is easy to get your basic ration coupons for petrol providing your car is already licensed. There was a brisk demand in Birmingham for basic ration petrol coupons, the issue of which began to-day, for vehicles already licensed, though there was nothing in the nature of a rush during the morning.

The British cruiser, HMS Birmingham, berthed in Copenhagen, May 1945.

P. 34 W. 34, goals for 269, against 26

I have received details of the outstanding football record of a Birmingham A.T.C. Squadron, 477 B.S.A.

During the season they played 34 matches and they won the lot, scoring 269 goals against 26.

Then the matches were not confined to Birmingham, for in winning the Sir Albert Ball Cup they came up against teams in the Midland Command. Their six matches in that competition yielded them 35 goals against six.

In winning the A.F.C. Cup (Birmingham Wing) they scored 44 goals against six in five matches, and the A.T.C. League Cup (South Division) yielded 63 goals against one in five matches.

James, the squadron's leading marksman, scored 91 goals in 22 appearances—an average of over four goals per match.

The pilot of an R.A.F. plane, of which he was believed to be the only occupant, was killed instantly when his machine crashed into a gorse-covered slope on the Lickey Hills, near Barnt Green, shortly after 9 o'clock this morning.

Identification of the pilot of the plane is difficult, as the machine burst into flames and was completely destroyed.

A youth working in the rickyard of the Yew Tree Farm, Lower Shepley, saw the plane dive low, apparently out of control and with smoke pouring from the engine. It buried itself in the ground and there were two loud explosions.

The youth ran to the spot and found the body of the pilot lying near a brook, with his parachute nearby.

Bromsgrove N.F.S. and police were called, and R.A.F. personnel took charge of the wreckage.

The new May Queen, Pauline Timerick, is crowned by her predecessor, Betty Hoyse, Tinkers Farm Secondary School, Northfield, 11th May 1945.

NEW GOVERNMENT CHOSEN

STATE of the Parties after the polling on July 5, 1945, and subsequently, was as follows : Two results remained to be announced. Labour registered a large majority over all other parties.

Conservative	—	—	—	200
National	—	—	—	2
Liberal National	—	—	—	13
Liberal	—	—	—	1

The foregoing represented the Nation's vote for the Government : total, 216.

Labour	—	—	—	393
Liberal	—	—	—	11
I.L.P.	—	—	—	3
Communist	—	—	—	2
Irish Nationalist	—	—	—	2
Common Wealth	—	—	—	1
Independent	—	—	—	8

Total for the Opposition, 420.

Gains and losses, as declared on July 26, were : Labour, 215 gains, 4 losses ; Conservative, 7 gains, 183 losses ; Liberals, 3 gains, 11 losses Thirty-two members of the Caretaker Government lost their seats. Of the Labour M.P.s 119 were trade unionists, half of them under 40, and 126 had come straight from the Services. Total of votes (which, all told, represented more than 75 per cent of the electorate) registered for Mr. Churchill's Government (July 26) was 10,075,283 ; against, 14,874,951.

Victor Yates, Labour MP for Ladywood, talks to Mrs Mary Hughes during his celebratory tour after winning the constituency, 1945.

VJ Day in Miller Street, Aston, 15th August 1945.

THE WARREN HILL RD.VICTORY FUND
BALANCE SHEET

INCOME	£.	s.	d.	EXPENDITURE	£.	s.	d	£.	s.	d
Cash C/F from VE Day		16.	7	CATERING						
Weekly Contributions	36.	19.	6	Mrs Enticknap	14.	1.	4½			
Collection Aug.15th	15.	19.	0	B'ham Dairy Co.	15.	0.	10			
" School Aug.16th	2.	8.	6	Cordials	3.	13.	6			
Donations	4.	16.	10	Ice Cream	1.	9.	0			
From Resale of Food	1.	7.	1½					34.	4.	8½
" " " Cordials	1.	1.	6	SPORTS				5.	0.	0
				Fancy Dress,Spot Prizes etc.	4.	0.	0			
	£63.	9.	0½	" Childrens		14.	0			
				Souvenirs				9.	15.	0
				Hall Hire	1.	10.	10			
				" Caretaker	1.	15.	0			
								3.	5.	10
				Lighting					7.	6
Signed ..D.C.Jones.. Auditor				Records 3 ea 4.2d					12.	6
				Stationary					3.	10
..D.Page..... Auditor				Balance. Cash in Hand				5.	5.	8
..A.Badsey... Secretary								£63.	9.	0½

Pupils at Glengarry Private School, High Street,
Harborne, 1945. The teacher is the Principal,
Miss Ethel Marshall.

WITH war production ending, British car manufacturers hope to double their target of 200,000 cars for this year.

Export trade will be the main consideration.

"Accumulated world demand must amount to at least £500,000,000," Mr. H. D. Simmons, of the Society of Motor Manufacturers and Traders, said yesterday.

"It is up to Britain to supply the cars.

"Our present target is only half normal peace output. We shall need to more than double it if all demands are to be met.

"Factories will be able to switch to civilian production very quickly. If demobilisation is speeded up there will be no shortage of labour.

"Providing there is no delay in releasing materials there is no need for unemployment in the motor industry."

Austin 10's being loaded onto an Avro-York, for exportation to South Africa, September 1945.

CRESCENT THEATRE MEMBERS

100 VACANCIES FOR 500 APPLICANTS

Only a short time after the announcement that it will re-open on September 22, the Crescent Theatre reports that so high a proportion of its pre-war members has rejoined that fewer than 100 vacancies are left for more than 500 new applicants.

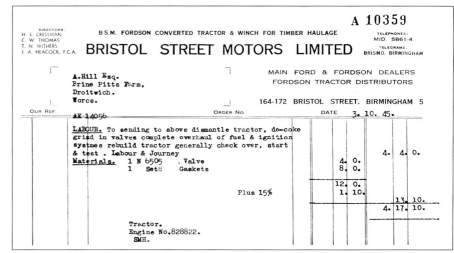

The King and Queen, accompanied by Princess Margaret, step ashore from HMS Birmingham, after an inspection of the Home Fleet, the Firth of Forth, 28th September 1945.

Will Fyffe, Scotland's great comedian, headlines the bill at the Hippodrome, 29th October 1945.

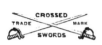

LUNCHEON

AT THE COUNCIL HOUSE

IN HONOUR OF THE
VISIT OF THEIR MAJESTIES
THE KING AND QUEEN

ALDERMAN W. T. WIGGINS-DAVIES J.P. LORD MAYOR

NOVEMBER 7TH 1945

The King and Queen arrive at the Accident Hospital, 7th November 1945.

1946

PRIME MINISTER'S APPEAL TO THE NATION'S WORKERS

TEAM SPIRIT TO WIN WAR AGAINST WANT

Broadcasting an appeal to the nation to work for more production, the Prime Minister on Sunday said: "I have not the slightest doubt that we shall come triumphantly through this testing time of 1946 just as we came through 1940." He said that work was the only way to get the goods so badly needed, and urged all classes to "march forward together cheerfully, to win the war against want."

Warmington Road residents' party,
Stanville Road Junior and Infants' School, Sheldon, 1946.

MINISTERS CONFER WITH EMPLOYERS

It was the turn of the nation's employers yesterday to go to Westminster to hear privately the Government's views on the man-power problem and the need for a production drive.

Wednesday's team of Mr. Attlee, Mr. Bevin and Mr. Isaacs was reinforced by Mr. Dalton, Chancellor of the Exchequer, and Sir Stafford Cripps, President of the Board of Trade. This indicated that the discussion embraced not only labour problems, but also those connected with official controls and restrictions of industry, finance and possibly taxation.

The conference of 1,700 delegates was arranged jointly by the British Employers Confederation and the Federation of British Industries.

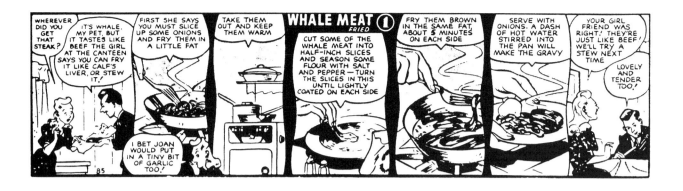

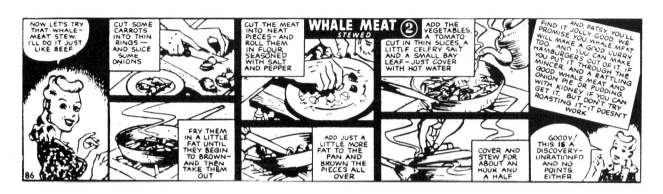

Handsworth Girls' Training Corps., 1946.

The bomb-damaged Metropole Cinema may re-open for stage shows, Snow Hill, 16th March 1946.

THE British farmer was called on in the Commons yesterday to make still greater efforts to produce food, and was offered some financial encouragement by the Government to do so.

Mr. T. Williams (Minister of Agriculture) told the House that in view of the world food crisis it was essential to plough up some land which had been laid down to seed when it was thought that more livestock and less cereals could safely be produced.

Rowheath Pavilion and Lido, 1946.

During a tour of factories, showing the different manufacturing industries housed in the city, organised by the Chamber of Commerce, the Lord Mayor, Ald. Alan Giles, chats to Mr. W. Macleod, Messrs. George Ellison Ltd. (switch gear manufacturers), Wellhead Lane, Perry Barr, 9th May 1946.

The newly-renovated drinking fountain in Temple Row, 1946.

- - CUT THIS OUT AND KEEP IT AS A GUIDE - - - - - -

How to get your new Ration Book

WHERE TO GO IN BIRMINGHAM
WHEN: 10th JUNE to 6th JULY, 1946

HOURS: Mondays to Fridays: 9 a.m. to 6.30 p.m.
Saturdays: 9 a.m. to 4. 0 p.m.

WEEK 3: 10th JUNE to 15th JUNE, 1946					
Mon.	Tues.	Wed.	Thurs.	Fri	Sat.
CLOSED	Ga-Go	Gr-Gz	Ha-Hi	Ho	Hu-Hz

Cen. No.	DISTRICT	DISTRIBUTION CENTRE
1	CITY	Civic Centre
2	ASTON	Victoria Road Baths
3	BALSALL HEATH	Moseley Road Baths
4	ERDINGTON	Mason Road, Erdington
5	HANDSWORTH	Grove Lane Baths
6	HARBORNE	Harborne Baths
7	KING'S HEATH	King's Heath Baths, Institute Road
8	KINGSTANDING	Kingstanding Baths, Warren Farm Rd.
9	LADYWOOD	Monument Road Baths
10	NORTHFIELD	Northfield Baths, Bristol Rd. South
11	SALTLEY	George Arthur Road Baths
12	SMALL HEATH	Green Lane Baths
13	SPARKHILL	Sparkhill Baths, Stratford Road
14	YARDLEY	Church Road Schools

Any person who attend a Distribution Centre may collect Ration Books for others outside the alphabetical range allotted for the day.
Every effort should be made to call on the day allotted to the particular letter to avoid queues and congestion.
Factories, Firms, and large organisations may, as in previous years, participate in the "Block Scheme" by arranging in writing direct with the Food Executive Officer. All envelopes should be marked at the top left-hand corner "Block Scheme."

VICTORY CELEBRATION

BIRMINGHAM DISCUSSIONS

Discussion is taking place among the chairmen of the main committees of Birmingham City Council and the principal officers of the Corporation as to the best means of celebrating victory on Whit-Saturday, June 8.

They met on Monday, under the chairmanship of the Lord Mayor, and discussed the general question on the basis of a circular from the Home Office, which outlined what is to be done in London—a victory parade of the Services, entertainments in public parks, concerts for the aged in public institutions, firework displays, and the illumination of public buildings.

A BRIGHTER CITY

NEED FOR PROVISION OF MORE AMUSEMENTS

ACCOMMODATION PROBLEM AT HOTELS

Some time may elapse before Birmingham people cease to go early to bed for lack of amusement, and some time before the city's hotels and restaurants can join in providing late night entertainment; but brighter Birmingham is on the way, and it has the blessing of the municipal authorities.

So much is clear from the conference on Birmingham's hotel problem, which was held under the chairmanship of the Lord Mayor of Birmingham at the Council House on Friday.

It was attended by representatives of the hotel business, railway and road transport, the Chamber of Commerce, and the licensing justices.

The most pressing need is the provision of more hotel accommodation for business men visiting the city. The conference, while going into this question, reviewed the whole problem of Birmingham's entertainment facilities and in large measure agreed that a considerable brightening of the city's " night life " is needed

SUNDAY, 9 JUNE, 1946.

LET US BE OF GOOD CHEER!

THE morning after the day before finds us perhaps wondering what it was all about. What we celebrated yesterday, with various degrees of enthusiasm, was not so much Victory as the defeat of a menace to freedom. There is not much for us to be cheerful about these days, but yesterday's occasion did at least provide a break in the monotonous gloom. We in these islands are badly in need of relief from sameness, and if we can work up a little brightness for ourselves, as most of us did yesterday, so much the better. We ought to get together more often in these victorious days of austerity and try to get a communal laugh out of our sorry mess.

The Council House is floodlit as part of the countrywide ongoing celebrations, 8th June 1946.

Warwickshire C.C.C., Summer 1946.

LAST-MINUTE rushes for the London trains, followed by an unexpected lull, show that while Birmingham found the celebrations in the capital a big attraction, the city's main favour is a holiday at home.

Rail and bus officials were surprised yesterday to find so few people travelling.

"Considerably less than the usual holiday Saturday and less, even, than a normal Saturday," was a Midland Red official's report on the company's traffic.

On the railways, after one train had left Snow Hill for Paddington in three parts with the third carrying 750 people, yesterday brought a lull described by one traffic controller as amazing.

"Long distance travel, which we expected to draw the crowds, was very little differnt from a normal summer Saturday," he said.

Seats were available in most trains as they left Birmingham, although one to Llandudno and another to Bristol and the West were crowded.

Little demand

There was little demand for transport to the nearer holiday centres, but in anticipation of bigger crowds to-day and to-morrow additional trains have been arranged for such destinations as Evesham, Stratford, Sutton, Malvern, and Ludlow.

Racing at Wolverhampton to-morrow—the first time for six years—is also expected to produce a big exodus from Birmingham.

Birmingham Transport Department had extra crews standing by ready to run relief buses, but traffic was very light

BEGINNING ON JULY 21, 1946, rationing of bread, flour, and flour confectionery in Britain was announced by the Minister of Food in the House of Commons on June 27. Mr. Strachey stated that the Government had reached this decision because they were convinced that to fail to ration bread and flour would be to take an unjustifiable risk with the basic foodstuff of the British people. In the subsequent Parliamentary debates, Mr. Strachey disclosed that there was no great reserve store of wheat lying idle in the country; there was only the stock going through the "pipe-line" from ships to shops. It was estimated that at the end of August there would be some eight weeks' supply of bread and flour in hand—sufficient to satisfy with certainty the bread supply of the country if a system of rationing were introduced, but not without it. Rationing enabled the authorities to work with a considerably smaller amount in the pipe-line. The basic adult ration is 9 oz. a day, with graduated amounts for children and extra allowances for manual workers

The Austin Motor Co., Longbridge, 1946.

✶

CAN Birmingham produce a girl vocalist with a voice to suit Roy Fox?

ROY, who has just come to England from New York, has not found the young lady yet.

OVER 100 girls think they have a chance to make a name for themselves, and are ready to prove it.

ON their voices and good looks depend their chances at the Grand Casino, Birmingham, auditions tomorrow.

NORTH of England towns have had their chance, but no new microphone personality has been found.

EIGHT years have passed since Roy Fox's famous "whispering" trumpet was heard in this country.

RADIO listeners will therefore, in the near future, probably be hearing a Birmingham girl on the air with him.

SO sing up, girls!

Bandleader, Roy Fox, attends the auditions at the Grand Casino, 3rd July 1946.

Open air dancing in Muntz Park, Umberslade Road, Selly Park, 25th July 1946.

THOUSANDS of animals and birds who played their part in the War were represented in London's Victory March, on June 8, 1946, by the Alsatians Jet and Irma. (See illus. in page 168.) These two Civil Defence Rescue Dogs, who wear the Dickin Medal—the Animals V.C.—for rescue work in air raids, are members of the Allied Forces Mascot Club of the People's Dispensary for Sick Animals. This club was formed to obtain lasting recognition for all the animals who, besides actual war work, contributed so much in maintaining moral and giving companionship to men and women of the Allied Forces.

THE Allied Forces Mascot Club, as well as compiling records for the Imperial War Museum of the wartime work of transport animals, guard and rescue dogs and homing pigeons, wishes to commemorate in a practical manner those who lost their lives. An Animals' War Memorial is to take the form of Caravan Dispensaries to bring relief to sick and suffering animals. Used throughout the War as rescue vehicles for thousands of animal raid victims, many such caravans were damaged or worn out, and the P.D.S.A. hopes to replace them by means of the Memorial funds which are now being raised by public subscription.

OF the 996 commissioned U-boats (German, Italian and Japanese) destroyed by the Allies throughout all the oceans of the world (said Mr. A. V. Alexander on March 7, 1946) over 300, or nearly one-third, were within 500 miles of the U.K.— this showing the intensity of the U-boats' concentration against the British Isles.

THE two outstanding months of the war against the U-boat were May 1943, when 46 U-boats were sunk, and April 1945, when the Germans were evacuating the Baltic ports and 65 U-boats were sent down. The month of May proved the turning-point of the war at sea : losses of Allied and neutral shipping, which averaged well over 20,000 tons daily in 1942 and over 14,000 tons daily in March-May 1943, fell by June-August to under 7,000 tons, and subsequently even lower.

IN the whole course of the war (it was stated on March 7, 1946) nearly 51,000 officers and men of the Royal Navy, including the Navies of the Dominions, and of the Royal Marines, were killed or were still missing. This number exceeded by over 20,000 the numbers killed between 1914-1918. Up to the end of 1945 nearly 15,000 awards had been made to officers and men of the Royal Navy, including the Dominion Navies, Royal Marines and Reserves ; these included 23 V.C.s and 29 G.C.s.

FROM the beginning of the war to August 31, 1945, H.M. ships and craft lost amounted to 3,282. The figure included three battleships and two battle cruisers, or one-third of our capital ship strength at the outbreak of the war ; five fleet carriers ; 23 cruisers ; 134 destroyers ; 77 submarines.

PEACE stamps, to commemorate the Victory celebrations, were on sale at British post-offices on June 11, 1946, when it was expected that the special issue of 264,000,000 would be exhausted in about two months. The total cash value of £2,800,000 is made up of 240,000,000 of the 2½d. denomination and 24,000,000 of the 3d. They are not available in book form, their size being double that of the ordinary stamp. The 2½d. one is blue, its design emphasizing peace through victory and reconstruction at home. The 3d. stamp, deep violet, symbolizes peace abroad. His Majesty the King made the final selection of the designs. See illus. below.

University of Birmingham, Edgbaston, c 1946.

Members of the Sparta team due to play Birmingham City at St. Andrew's on Monday are (left to right) standing: Blaha, Ludl, Koubek, Riha, Ceip, Kokstein, Zastera ; kneeling: Zmatlik, Senecky, Horak, Vejvoda.

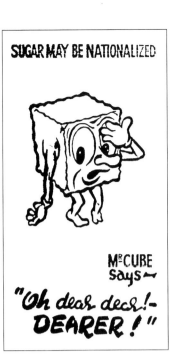

SUGAR MAY BE NATIONALIZED

Mr CUBE says—

"Oh dear deer!—
DEARER!"

The family gathering to celebrate the Golden Wedding of Mr and Mrs Edward Cadbury,
Bournville, 22nd October 1946.

The Rt. Hon. Aneurin Bevan, Minister of Health, addresses the audience at the prize-giving evening at the
Queen Elizabeth Hospital, Edgbaston, 1st November 1946.

A group of semi-final winners in the Carrol Levis talent competition, Midland Institute, 5th January 1947.

Trevor Ford, transferred from Swansea Town to Aston Villa at a fee of £10,000, January 1947.

Mobile Police Station, Duke Street, Gosta Green, 20th January 1947.

Freddie Mills.

The Birmingham Mail Christmas Tree Fund

CHARITY BOXING TOURNAMENT

Thimblemill Lane, Smethwick

THURSDAY, 13th FEBRUARY, 1947

UNDER THE PATRONAGE OF THE WORSHIPFUL THE MAYOR (Alderman Mrs. E. M. Farley, J.P.)

The Match Birmingham has been waiting for!
10 3-MINUTE ROUND LIGHT-WEIGHT CONTEST:

BILLY BIDDLES v. ALF EDWARDS

Birmingham (lost 4 professional fights out of 50)   Smethwick (lost 2 fights since coming out of Services)

8 3-MINUTE ROUND WELTER-WEIGHT CONTEST:

JACK PHILLIPS   v.   DOUG BYGRAVE

Tradeser (recently boxed Henry Hall to a close decision)   Norwich (Freddie Mills Sparring Partner. Met most of the best)

FREDDIE MILLS

(Light Heavy-weight Champion of Great Britain.   Lonsdale Belt Holder)

Will box Training bout with selected opponents

4 3-MINUTE ROUND HEAVY-WEIGHT CONTEST:

DANNY SEWELL   v.   WALLY CORBETT

London (Ted Broadribb's 17 year old sensation)   Porth (young Welshman who will give Sewell the acid test)

8 3-MINUTE ROUND LIGHT-WEIGHT CONTEST:

CHRIS JENKINS   v.   ARTHUR BENTON

Bucks bridge (Won 6 of 6 professional contests)   Birmingham (Has beaten Jimmy Brown, Al Rex, Tony McGowan, Jim O'Leary, Larry Benson)

8 3-MINUTE ROUND WELTER-WEIGHT CONTEST:

BILL CADBY v. REG HOBLIN

Birmingham (Has won all contests since leaving the Army by Knock-out. Can he continue this time?)   London (Has class record. Can he stop Cadby?)

All Seats Reserved.   £3 3s. 0d., £2 2s. 0d., £1 1s. 0d., 10s. 6d., 5s.

Referees appointed by B.B.B. of C.   All Officials Licence Holders   Buses pass the door.   Late buses to all parts

DOORS OPEN 6.30 P.M.   START 7.15 P.M. PROMPT.

Weigh-in at Blue Gates Hotel, Smethwick at 2 p.m. on the day

TICKETS MAY OBTAINED FROM :—

SUPERINTENDENT, Thimblemill Baths, Smethwick (BEA. 1421); JIM MURPHY, Farcroft Hotel, Rookery Rd., Handsworth (NOR. 0067); SID LEES, The Ivy Bush, Hagley Rd., Edgbaston (EDG. 9893); ALDERMAN C. H. MARRIOTT, J.P., 139, Oldbury Rd., Smethwick (SMR 0066); LEB TARRANT, Old House at Home, Halfords Lane, Smethwick; Mr. G. G. TIDSALL, The Midland Bank, High Street, Smethwick (SME. 1177); SYD WHARTON, High Street, Smethwick (SME. 1401) THE BIRMINGHAM POST & MAIL LTD., Cannon Street, Birmingham (MID 4461).

JOURNAL, Cannon Passage, Birmingham.

Chamberlain Square, from Ratcliff Place, March 1947.

The Bull Ring, looking towards Digbeth, March 1947.

The traffic turns from Hill Street into New Street
with great difficulty, 5th March 1947.

NOW most of Birmingham's snow has disappeared and the floods are on the wane, public works officials are facing a new problem—DIRT.

A formidable clearing-up job awaits the city's workmen, who for nearly two months have been unable to attempt "spring cleaning" of the streets.

An official said to-day that it will be a considerable time before things are normal again.

Reports from Birmingham railway officials, transport managers and public works authorities show, however, that public services are steadily improving.

Flood waters in Walsall-road area at Perry Barr, are receding rapidly, though some roads are still closed to traffic.

Water in Church-road has subsided, and it is open to outward-bound traffic, but diversions are still necessary for inward-bound traffic.

Hamstead Hill is still under water and closed for transport.

Both the L.M.S. and G.W.R. state that all local services are running normally and flooding is causing little inconvenience.

Yesterday the L.M.S. moved 11,000 tons of coal from Cannock Chase collieries.

THEATRES AND CINEMAS

THEATRE ROYAL NEW STREET. B'HAM.
Matinees Daily (Tues. & Fri. excepted) 2.0 p.m. Evenings at 7.0 p.m.
TOM ARNOLD & EMILE LITTLER present
GOODY TWO SHOES
FRED EMNEY
JOY HAYDEN HENRY LYTTON
JACK STANFORD SMEDDLE BROS.
CAST OF 80 ARTISTES.
Box Office Open 10 a.m. until 8.30 p.m.

ALEXANDRA THEATRE
MATS. 2 (Fri. exc.), EVNGS. 7 p.m.
SIMPLE SIMON
Mar. 31: KEEP IT DARK, a new Farce. Prior to London Production.
Apl. 7: POLISH PARADE. A Medley of Music, Ballet and Song.
Apl. 14: "WE PROUDLY PRESENT." A new Play by Ivor Novello.
Apl. 21: BALLETS JOOSS.
Apl. 28 (to be announced).
Box Office for above open 20/3/47
May 5: Opening of Repertory Season.

REPERTORY THEATRE.
Evenings (ex. Mon.) 6.30. Matinees Wednesday, Thursday, Saturday, 2.30.
Sir Barry Jackson presents
"THE SILENT WOMAN,"
By Ben Jonson.
Box Office 10.30—7. No phone bookings.
Tuesday, April 1st: "AN IDEAL HUSBAND," by Oscar Wilde.

HIPPODROME
HURST STREET, B'HAM.
6.0. TWICE NIGHTLY. 8.15.
ARTHUR ASKEY
EDDIE GRAY
VICTOR BARNA & ALEC BROOK.
THE CYCLING D'ORMONDES.
NOR KIDDIE. JANET BROWN.
MARY PRIESTMAN.
CYNTHIA & GLADYS.
THE JAVA BROTHERS.
Box Office Open 10.0 a.m. until 9.0 p.m.

ASTON HIPPODROME
6.20 — TWICE NIGHTLY — 8.30
The Man Who Invented Shakespeare.
LEON CORTEZ
of B.B.C. "HARMONY HALL."
With SPECIAL APPEARANCE of
ARTHUR WHITE
in "VARIETY FAIR."

DUDLEY AMUSEMENTS

DUDLEY HIPPODROME
Nightly at 7.30. Mat. Sat. at 4.15 p.m.
Last Performance Saturday, Mar. 22nd.
S. H. NEWSOME presents
JACK & THE BEANSTALK.
JACK EDGE. :: ROY ROYSTON.
Mon., March 24th—Nightly at 7.30.
Mats. Wed. and Thurs., 2.15 p.m.—
"THE STUDENT PRINCE."
Box Office Open 10.0 a.m. until 9.0 p.m.

COVENTRY AMUSEMENTS

HIPPODROME, COVENTRY.
(Phone 3141). This Week and Next Week. Evenings 6.45. Matinees Thursday and Saturday, 2.30.
THE ROYAL CARL ROSA OPERA, under direction of H. B. Phillips.
Repertoire details apply Box Office.
Sun., March 23rd, 7.0 p.m.: New Midlands Philharmonic Orchestra. Conductor, Mathew Stevenson; Phyllis Sellick and Cyril Smith.
Mar. 31: Evgs. 6.45. Mats. Thurs., Sat., 2.30: 'LADY WINDERMERE'S FAN.'

WEDNESBURY AMUSEMENTS

WEDNESBURY HIPPODROME
(Phone WED. 0634).
Nightly at 7.15 p.m. Saturday 6 and 8.15 p.m.
THE MAGNET REPERTORY CO. in
MA'S BIT O' BRASS.
A Comedy by Ronald Gow.
FREE CAR PARK.

AMUSEMENTS

ICE SKATING RINK,
SUMMER HILL ROAD. CEN. 6036.
At 11.0, 2.30, and 7.30.
BOOTS AND SKATES NOW AVAILABLE FOR HIRE.

ODEON THEATRE, Warley.
SUNDAY, MARCH 23rd. NAT ALLEN WITH HIS RADIO AND TELEVISION ORCHESTRA, with NANETTE REES & JUDY DEAN.
Doors Open 6.30. Com. 7 p.m. Book Now.

ODEON NEW-STREET.
Doors Open 10.0 a.m. Continuous until 10.30 p.m.
TEMPTATION (A)
with
MERLE OBERON,
GEORGE BRENT,
CHARLES KORVIN, PAUL LUKAS.
Screened at 11.35, 2.46, 5.57, 8.58.
Also
MR. BIG (U)
DONALD O'CONNOR,
GLORIA JEAN,
PEGGY RYAN, ROBERT PAIGE.
Screened at 10.25, 1.24, 4.35, 7.46.

GAUMONT STEELHOUSE LANE
Continuous from 12.30 p.m.
DANNY KAYE
VIRGINIA MAYO
VERA-ELLEN
in
THE KID FROM BROOKLYN (u)
With the Gorgeous Goldwyn Girls (In Technicolor)
At 1.50, 5.10 and 8.25.
CANDY'S CALENDAR (U)
At 12.50, 4.10, and 7.25
MARCH OF TIME No. 1 — New Series (u)

FORUM Cont. 12.35. MID. 4549.
An A.B.C. Theatre.
SECOND BIG WEEK OF
CARY GRANT
ALEXIS SMITH
in Cole Porter's
NIGHT AND DAY (U)
in Glorious Technicolor.
with
MONTY WOOLLEY GINNY SIMMS
MARY MARTIN JANE WYMAN
Screened at 12.55, 3.20, 5.50, 8.15.
To-morrow Continuous from 12.35 p.m.

WEST END. —— MID. 0022.
DOORS OPEN 11.45. COMM. 12.0 noon.
GRAND ALL-BRITISH PROGRAMME
JOHN MILLS,
VALERIE HOBSON,
BERNARD MILES
in
GREAT EXPECTATIONS (A)
introducing
ANTHONY WAGER. JEAN SIMMONS.
Showing at 12.0, 2.50, 5.40, 8.30.
FULL SUPPORTING PROGRAMME.
At Your Service—The West End Cafe.

FUTURIST THEATRE
To-day
RAY MILLAND,
TERESA WRIGHT
in
MRS. LORING'S SECRET (A)
2.0, 5.10, 8.15
also
FREDDIE STEWART,
JUNE PREISSER
in
FREDDIE STEPS OUT (A)
12.50, 3.55, 7.0

SCALA TO-DAY
CONSTANCE MOORE,
WILLIAM MARSHALL
in
HATS OFF TO RHYTHM (U)
12.30, 3.10, 5.50, 8.25
also
DONALD BARRY, ANN SAVAGE
in
THE LAST CROOKED MILE (A)
2.5, 4.45, 7.25

TATLER THEATRE STATION STREET
CONTINUOUS FROM 10.15 A.M.
PRICES 10d. AND 1/6.
DUTCH VISTA

CINEMATOGRAPH EXHIBITORS' ASSOCIATION

ADELPHI, Hay Mills (A.B.C.). VIC. 1208. John Loder, Lenore Aubert, **THE WIFE OF MONTE CRISTO** (A). Also **JOE PALOOKA, CHAMP** (A).

ALBION, New Inns, HANDSWORTH.—**SEND FOR PAUL TEMPLE** (A), Anthony Hulme, Joy Shelton; **HOW DO YOU DO-O-O?** (U), Bert Gordon.

ALHAMBRA, Moseley-rd (A.B.C.). VIC. 2826. Anna Lee, James Ellison in **G.I. WAR BRIDES** (U); and Albert Dekker, **THE FRENCH KEY** (a). News.

APOLLO —— TYBURN ROAD. Randolph Scott in **BAD MAN'S TERRITORY** (U), Etc. Thursday: Magic Bow (u).

ASTORIA, Aston (A.B.C.). AST. 2384. Claudette Colbert, **WITHOUT RESERVATIONS** (A); supported by Philip Reed in **BIG TOWN** (A). News.

ATLAS, STECHFORD. —— STE. 2206. **THE CHINESE BUNGALOW** (A), Kay Walsh, Paul Lukas; **THE MAN WHO LOST HIMSELF** (U), K. Francis.

BEACON —— GREAT BARR. Edward G. Robinson, **THE SEA WOLF** (A). 2.20, 5.30, 8.40; **The Shadow Returns** (a). Thurs: Miss Susie Slagles

BEACON, Smethwick (A.B.C.). SME. 1045. EPIC OF ARNHEM, **THEIRS IS THE GLORY** (A). Full Supporting Programme.

BEAUFORT, WASHWOOD HEATH.—David Niven, Roger Livesey, Raymond Massey, **A MATTER OF LIFE AND DEATH** (A). Sun: This is the Life (a)

BIRCHFIELD, Perry Barr. BIR. 4333. Pat O'Brien and Ruth Warwick in **Perilous Holiday** (a); **Faithful in My Fashion** (a). Thurs: Michael Strogoff.

BRISTOL, Bristol-road (A.B.C.). CAL. 1904. Robert Donat, Emlyn Williams, **THE CITADEL** (A); Kent Taylor, **Deadline for Murder** (a).

BROADWAY, Bristol-street. MID. 1761. ANNA LEE, JAMES ELLISON in **G.I. WAR BRIDES** (A), and **FRENCH KEY** (A).

CAPITOL, WARD END.—Rex Harrison, Diana Churchill in **SCHOOL FOR HUSBANDS** (A); Laurel and Hardy in **FLYING DEUCES** (U).

CARLTON, SPARKBROOK. SOU. 0861. STEWART GRANGER, PHYLLIS CALVERT in **THE MAGIC BOW** (U). Full supporting programme.

CASTLE BROMWICH CINEMA. — Karen Morley, Jim Bannon, Jeff Donnell in **THE UNKNOWN** (A); also **Blondie Knows Best** (U).

CLIFTON —— GREAT BARR. **A MATTER OF LIFE AND DEATH** (A) (Tech.) 5.40, 8.20. Full Support. Sun.: Higher and Higher (U).

CORONET, SMALL HEATH. VIC. 0420. Olivia De Havilland, Lew Ayres, **THE DARK MIRROR** (A); **THE BAXTER MILLIONS** (U), Fay Holden.

CROWN, Ladywood (A.B.C.). EDG. 1122. Paul Kelly, Douglas Fowley, **GLASS ALIBI** (A); Philip Reed and Hilary Brook, **BIG TOWN** (A). News.

DANILO, LONGBRIDGE. PRI. 2470. Betty Hutton in **CROSS MY HEART** (A) at 2.15, 5.35, 9.0; Will Fyffe in **Rulers of the Sea** (U) at 3.45, 7.10.

DANILO, QUINTON. WOO 2562.—Michael Wilding in **CARNIVAL** (A), with Sally Gray; also **CLUB HAVANA** (A).

EDGBASTON, Monument-road (A.B.C.). EDG. 3273. Van Johnson & Keenan Wynn. **NO LEAVE NO LOVE** (U); also **CHILDREN ON TRIAL** (A).

ELITE —— HANDSWORTH NOR. 0665. For Six Days. Birmingham's Own Hazel Court, Michael Wilding in **CARNIVAL** (A).

EMPIRE, SMETHWICK. SME. 0757. John Loder, Lenore Aubert in **THE WIFE OF MONTE CRISTO** (A); also Tom Neal in **CLUB HAVANA** (A).

GAIETY, COLESHILL ST. (A.B.C.). CEN. 6649. **WEEK-END IN HAVANA** (U), in Colour; **RENDEZVOUS 24** (A).

EMPRESS, Sutton (A.B.C.). Sut. 2363. Robert Donat, Emlyn Williams in **THE CITADEL** (A), And Full Supporting Programme.

ERA CINEMA, BORDESLEY GREEN. Robert Young, Helen Gilbert, Lee Bowman, and Charles Coburn in **FLORIAN** (U).

GLOBE, ASTON. —— AST. 0652. John Wayne in **DAKOTA** (A). **HANDS ACROSS THE OCEAN** (U).

GRAND, Soho-road, HANDSWORTH.—**FLIGHT FROM FOLLY** (A), Pat Kirkwood, Sydney Howard; also **ELMER'S OTHER TALE** (A).

GRAND, Alum Rock-road, SALTLEY. **THE LAST OUTPOST** (A), Cary Grant; **DOUBLE EXPOSURE** (A), Chester Morris.

GRANGE, SMALL HEATH. VIC. 0434. Rex Harrison, Diana Churchill in **SCHOOL FOR HUSBANDS** (A); Laurel and Hardy in **FLYING DEUCES** (U).

GROVE CINEMA, Dudley-road. SME. 0343. **The Dark Mirror** (a), Mon. to Fri. 3.17, 6.4, 8.51; **The Baxter Millions** (u) Sun: Woman of the Town (a).

IMPERIAL, Moseley-rd. (A.B.C.). CAL. 2283. Rex Harrison, **ANNA AND THE KING OF SIAM** (A), with Irene Dunne, also **GLAMOUR GIRL** (A).

KING'S NORTON— June Haver, **THREE LITTLE GIRLS IN BLUE** (U); Philip Reed, **BIG TOWN** (A).

KINGSTON, SMALL HEATH. VIC. 2639. George Raft and Sylvia Sidney, in **MR. ACE** (A); also William Boyd, in **LUMBERJACK** (U).

KINGSWAY —— HIG. 1352. June Haver, George Montgomery, in **THREE LITTLE GIRLS IN BLUE** (U) (Tech.). Screened at 2.25, 5.35, 8.45.

LUXOR.—Gene Tierney, Cornel Wilde, **LEAVE HER TO HEAVEN** (A) (Technicolor). FULL SUPPORT.

LYRIC, PARADE. —**SMOKEY** (U) (Technicolor), Fred MacMurray, Anne Baxter; **LUCKY CISCO KID** (U), Cesar Romero.

MAJESTIC, BEARWOOD.—Mon.—Fri. 6, Sat. 5. Barbara Stanwyck, **THE BRIDE WORE BOOTS** (A); also **BIG TOWN** (A).

MAYFAIR —— PERRY COMMON. **OLD MOTHER RILEY AT HOME** (A) and **ENCHANTED ISLE.** Thurs.: Courage of Lassie (a).

MAYPOLE, King's Heath. WAR. 2051. Betty Grable, June Haver, in **THE DOLLY SISTERS** (A) (in Technicolor).

NORTHFIELD CINEMA. PRI. 1463.—Lee Bowman, **The Walls Came Tumbling Down** (a); **Personality Kid** (u). Thurs.: Claudia and David (a).

OAK, Selly Oak (A.B.C.). SEL. 0139. Bruce Bennett, **TARZAN AND THE GREEN GODDESS** (U); supported by Laurel and Hardy in **JAILBIRDS** (U).

ODEON, BLACKHEATH. BLA. 1036. Janet Blair, **TARS AND SPARS** (U) James Craig, **DANGEROUS PARTNERS** (A).

ODEON —— KINGSTANDING. **WIFE OF MONTE CRISTO** (A). **JUST WILLIAM** (U). (Last Performance 7.30 p.m.)

ODEON, PERRY BARR. BIR. 4453.—**THE PERFECT MARRIAGE** (A) Also **MEN WITH WINGS** (U). Last Complete Performance 7 p.m.

ODEON, SHIRLEY —— SHI. 1183. Cont. 2.0 p.m. Johnny Weissmuller, Brenda Joyce, **TARZAN & THE AMAZONS** (U). **One Way To Love** (u).

ODEON, SUTTON COLDFIELD.—Michael Redgrave, **The Years Between** (a). Last Perf. 7.15. Thurs.: The Perfect Marriage (a).

ODEON —— WARLEY. David Niven, **THE PERFECT MARRIAGE** (A), 2.15, 5.33, 8.51. **Men With Wings** (u). Last Perf 7.0.

OLTON CINEMA.—Tom Walls, Glynis Johns, Jeanne de Casalis, **THIS MAN IS MINE** (A). With Full Support.

OLYMPIA, LADYPOOL-RD. VIC. 0124. Ralph Richardson, Edna Best, **SOUTH RIDING** (A). Sidney Toler, **THE JADE MASK** (A).

ORIENT, Aston (A.B.C.). NOR. 1615. Walter Pidgeon, Jane Powell in **HOLIDAY IN MEXICO** (U). Colour. And Full Supporting Programme.

PALACE, Erdington (A.B.C.). ERD. 1623. Robert Donat, Emlyn Williams, **THE CITADEL** (A) And Full Supporting Programme.

PALLADIUM, Hockley (A.B.C.). NOR. 0380. Karen Morley, Jim Bannon in **THE UNKNOWN** (A), Also **THE MAN WHO DARED** (A).

PAVILION, STIRCHLEY (A.B.C.). KIN. 1241. Walter Pidgeon, Jane Powell, **HOLIDAY IN MEXICO** (U). Colour. And Full Supporting Programme.

PAVILION, Wylde Green (A.B.C.). ERD. 0224. Walter Pidgeon, Jane Powell, **HOLIDAY IN MEXICO** (U). Colour. And Full Supporting Programme.

PICCADILLY, Sparkbrook (A.B.C.). VIC. 1688. Bruce Bennett, **TARZAN AND THE GREEN GODDESS** (U); Laurel and Hardy, **FLYING DEUCES** (U).

PICTURE HOUSE, Aston Cross (A.B.C.). EAS. 0430. Sydney Greenstreet in **THE VERDICT** (A); and also **ONE EXCITING WEEK** (A).

PICTURE HOUSE, Erdington (A.B.C.). ERD. 1484. Edward G. Robinson in **THE STRANGER** (A). Also **RADIO STARS ON PARADE** (A).

PICTURE HOUSE (G.B.), HARBORNE. All Week: David Niven, Kim Hunter, in **A MATTER OF LIFE & DEATH** (A) (Tech.), the Royal Command Film!

PLAZA, Stockland Green. ERD. 1048. David Niven, **MATTER OF LIFE & DEATH** (A); **CRIMSON CANARY** (A). Sunday: Behind the Rising Sun (a).

PRINCES, SMETHWICK. SME. 0221. Anna Neagle and Michael Wilding in **PICCADILLY INCIDENT** (A); also **WOMEN IN SPORT** (U).

REGAL, Handsworth (A.B.C.). NOR. 1801. Walter Pidgeon, Jane Powell, **HOLIDAY IN MEXICO** (U). Colour. And Full Supporting Programme.

RIALTO, HALL GREEN. SPR. 1270. **The Adventures of Robin Hood** (u), Errol Flynn, Olivia de Havilland, Basil Rathbone. Full Support Programme (u).

RINK (G.B.), Smethwick. SME. 0950. Ingrid Bergman, **ADAM HAD FOUR SONS** (A); **DANGEROUS BUSINESS** (A). Free Car Park for Patrons.

RITZ, Bordesley Green (A.B.C.). VIC. 1070. Ida Lupino, Robert Alda in **THE MAN I LOVE** (A); Anne Gwynne, **I RING DOORBELLS** (A).

ROBIN HOOD, Hall Green (A.B.C.). SPR. 2371. Walter Pidgeon, Jane Powell, **HOLIDAY IN MEXICO** (U). (Tech.). Full supporting programme.

ROCK CINEMA, Alum Rock.—Chips Rafferty and Daphne Campbell in **THE OVERLANDERS** (U); **CLUB HAVANA** (A). Thurs.: Carnival (a).

ROYALTY, Harborne (A.B.C.). HAR. 1619. Douglas Fairbanks, **CORSICAN BROTHERS** (A); Dennis O'Keefe, **GETTING GERTIE'S GARTER** (A).

RUBERY CINEMA. Phone 193.—Bela Lugosi, Lon Chaney, in **Frankenstein Meets the Wolf Man** (H); **Easy to Look At** (U). No children under 16 admitted

SAVOY, King's Norton. KIN. 1069.—Alan Ladd, Loretta Young, **AND NOW TO-MORROW** (A); John Carradine in **FACE OF MARBLE** (A).

SHELDON CINEMA —— SHE. 2158. Humphrey Bogart, Lauren Bacall in **THE BIG SLEEP** (A). Thurs.: CLAUDIA AND DAVID (A).

SOLIHULL —— SOL. 0398 Anthony Hulme and Joy Shelton in **SEND FOR PAUL TEMPLE** (A); **Blossoms in the Dust** (a) Greer Garson

STAR CINEMA, Erdington. EAS. 0461. **SEND FOR PAUL TEMPLE** (A), Anthony Hulme; **Come Out Fighting** (a) **East Side Kids.** Thurs: Devotion (u)

TIVOLI PLAYHOUSE, Coventry-road.—**THE PHANTOM** (A) with Tom Tyler, Jeanne Bates; **OUR HEARTS WERE GROWING UP** (A), Gail Russell.

TUDOR, KING'S HEATH (A.B.C.). HIG. 1161. Ida Lupino, Robert Alda, in **THE MAN I LOVE** (A); Anne Crawford in **HEADLINE** (A).

TRIANGLE, Gooch-street, Birmingham. **JUST BEFORE THE DAWN** (A) Warner Baxter; also **HIT THE HAY** (A), Judy Canova.

VICTORIA. EAS 0479. — Paulette Goddard, Ray Milland in **KITTY** (A); **THEY MADE ME A KILLER** (A). Thurs.: G.I. WAR BRIDES (U).

VILLA CROSS (G.B.). NOR. 0607. — The Royal Command Performance Film. David Niven in **A MATTER OF LIFE & DEATH** (A) (Tech.) 3.20, 6.0, 8.35.

WARWICK CINEMA, Acock's Green. Louis Hayward, Joan Bennett, Warren William, Alan Hale in **THE MAN IN THE IRON MASK** (A).

WEOLEY —— WEOLEY CASTLE George Raft, Joan Bennett, **The House Across The Bay** (A); **Texas Masquerade** (U). Mon. & Thurs. Cont. from 2.30.

WINDSOR, BEARWOOD. BEA 2244. Mon., Thurs., Sat. from 5. Tues., Wed., Fri. 6. Maureen O'Hara, **Spanish Main** (A); also **Scottish Symphony** (U).

WINSON GREEN. NORTHERN 1790. **Her Kind of Man** (A), Zachary Scott; **So Dark the Night** (A), **Steve Geray.** Thurs.: Devotion (U). Ida Lupino.

WEST BROMWICH CINEMAS

CLIFTON, STONE CROSS. STO. 2141. Boris Karloff, Lon Chaney, in **House of Frankenstein** (H). Children under 16 not admitted. **She Wrote the Book** (A)

IMPERIAL, West Bromwich. WES. 0192 David Niven, Kim Hunter, Roger Livesey, **A MATTER OF LIFE AND DEATH** (A) (Tech.), at 3.5, 5.40, 8.20

PALACE CINEMA. WES. 0358.—David Niven, Roger Livesey, **A MATTER OF LIFE & DEATH** (A) (Tech), approx. 2.40, 5.30, 8.15; **Land of the Saints** (u)

PLAZA, WEST BROMWICH. WES. 0030 Fred Astaire and Paulette Goddard in **SECOND CHORUS** (U); also Bill Boyd in **BORDERLAND** (U).

QUEEN'S. WES. 0351. Large Car Park. Paul Lukas and Jane Baxter in **THE CHINESE BUNGALOW** (A); Brian Aherne, **Man Who Lost Himself** (u).

ST. GEORGE'S CINEMA. Phone WES. 0737. Patricia Burke, David Farrar, Richard Tauber, in **THE LISBON STORY** (A).

TOWER (A.B.C.). —— WES. 1210. Cary Grant and Alexis Smith, **NIGHT AND DAY** (U). (Tech.). Life Story of Cole Porter.

The Lord Mayor, Ald. Albert Bradbeer, receives a greetings scroll, from a German prisoner-of-war, which he will convey to the Lord Mayor of Cologne. Maxstoke P.O.W. Camp, Coleshill, 31st March 1947.

The Chancellor of the Exchequer, Sir Stafford Cripps, meets dignitaries outside St Martin's, 12th May 1947.

The bearded actor, Trevor Howard, is greeted on his arrival, prior to making a personal appearance, at the Gaumont Cinema, Steelhouse Lane, 13th May 1947.

Broad Street, 1947.

The Birmingham Parks Department sets out to improve the lower part of Broad Street, by planting an attractive rock garden in front of the Municipal Bank, 13th May 1947.

Corporation Street, 7th June 1947.

A bit of a snarl-up looks imminent, at the junction of Albert Street and Moor Street, 16th June 1947.

Paralysis has reached new peak figure

LATEST Ministry of Health figures, issued yesterday, reveal that infantile paralysis cases in England and Wales reached a peak figure of 662 on September 6.

New notifications in the main towns were: London, 69; Birmingham, 28; Manchester, 15; Liverpool, 14; Sunderland, Leicester and Sheffield 10 each; Bradford 9; Croydon, Ealing, Bristol and Salford 8 each.

A Ministry of Health official said: "It must be expected that the figures will fluctuate for the time being.

"This is because the experience of other years showed that the number of cases tends to rise and fall intermittently until well into the autumn."

The Ministry state that one of the greatest single causes of the epidemic spreading is the failure of the general public to wash their hands.

Local authorities are being urged to provide towels, soap and hot water, free if possible, in public cloakrooms.

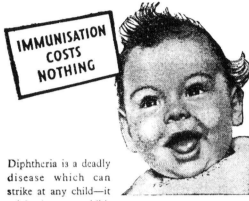

DIPHTHERIA COSTS LIVES

IMMUNISATION COSTS NOTHING

Diphtheria is a deadly disease which can strike at any child—it might be *your* child.

The figures show that a child who has been immunised is much less likely to catch diphtheria, and the chance that he will die from it is 26 times less than that of a child who has not been given protection.

Dare you take this risk? Every baby ought to be protected before he is a year old.

Ask at your Local Council Offices or Welfare Centre for advice.

Issued by the Ministry of Health and the
Central Council for Health Education

Adelaide Street/Charles Henry Street, c 1947.

St Martin's, Bull Ring, September 1947.

THIS week the Board of Trade will announce a cut in clothing coupons. At least four coupons are to be deducted from the present allocation of thirty-two, which ends next month.

The shock would have been greater still, the *Sunday Pictorial* was told yesterday, but for the fact that a great proportion of textiles for the next period have already been made up on Utility lines, and are not suitable for export.

By next March most textiles will have been prepared for export, leaving comparatively little for home use. There may, however, be concessions for children's clothing.

Thousands of demobbed Service men and women who are still owed twenty-six clothing coupons by the Board of Trade will get them in November, and details are to be announced next month.

Godfrey Winn, author of "Holiday Camp", surrounded by autograph hunters, at the West End Cinema, 19th September 1947. He was born in Woodbourne Road, Edgbaston.

Edwards Road/Orphanage Road, Erdington, 1947.

LIVING accommodation for transferred workers and Poles arriving to man basic industries is still a major headache in the Birmingham region. But first billets in an Apley Park hostel, secured primarily for local iron companies, have been assigned to a sugar beet firm. Industrialists are asking who blundered, and why?

THE details of a wedding that has aroused keen controversy are being arranged with wise caution, and its organisers are walking on tip-toes.

On November 20 Princess Elizabeth and Lieutenant Philip Mountbatten become man and wife. Precedent demands pomp and luxury for the wedding of our future Queen, and already there are signs of excitement and interest in the land.

Accommodation in London at the time of the wedding is now impossible. The Travel Association announce that hotels have been flooded with cables and letters from all parts of the world.

As was the case on Victory Day and Coronation Day, astronomical prices for seats in private buildings are being asked and obtained.

Undoubtedly the nation, with few extremist exceptions, is delighted that a popular princess has made a love match, but feelings on how the wedding should be conducted are divided.

Work's convener, Dick Etheridge, addresses a meeting of Austin workers, Longbridge, 1947.

RADIO HIGHLIGHTS

HOME

11.30 a.m., London String Orchestra. 3.0 p.m., Calvet String Quartet (Beethoven-Ravel). 4.10, "Perpetual Honeymoon," a radio fantasy. 6.40, Sunday Salon with Anton and his Orchestra. 9.15, the Battle for Britain, the full story of Hitler's plan for the invasion of Britain in 1940. 10.15, Sir Malcolm Sargent introduces "Gilbert and Sullivan."

LIGHT

10.30 a.m., Down Your Way (Bognor): 3.30 p.m., Battle of Britain Festival with George Robey and Vi Loraine. 5.0, Family Favourites. 6.0, Variety—with Ted Ray. 7.10, Carroll Levis Show (guest star: Walter Jackson). 8.15, Rainbow Room. Reg. Leopold's Orchestra, with Dorothy Pouishnoff (piano). 9.30, Richard Tauber programme (guest artist: Janet Davis).

NEW RECORDS FOR YOUR GRAMOPHONE

Recommended. Sydney Torch's orchestra in a selection from the evergreen "Merry Widow" (Parl. E 11455). "Tell Me, Marianne" and "The Stars Will Remember," neatly carolled by Monte Rey (Col. FB 3302). And the same singer in "Down the Old Spanish Trail" (Col. FB 3321), backed by "Mia Canzon' d'Amore."

A new sweeper-collector machine, recently put into operation by the Public Works Department of Birmingham Corporation, collects more than a ton of litter per mile, even in suburban districts. Along the Bristol Road, between Priory Road and Oak Tree Lane, four tons 5cwt. of rubbish was collected on one trip.

Birmingham Corporation's salvage department daily screens the city's waste for recoverable materials, and the war-time scheme is still in operation for the collection of waste paper—which should be put out for the dustmen in separate packages. Private enterprise, too, works effectively to collect waste paper for re-pulping.

B'HAM AGAIN LEADS

With a total of all categories of 5,286 houses built up to the end of August, Birmingham once more leads the county boroughs listed in the Ministry of Health's latest returns issued to-day. Coventry, with 2,515, drops to sixth place.

Birmingham's total is made up of 932 new houses completed since the war under the Corporation's schemes, with 222 rebuilt war-destroyed homes and 2,763 temporary houses provided by the Ministry of Works. Private enterprise was responsible for 951 new houses and 418 rebuilds. These figures give a total for the Corporation of 1,154 and 1,369 for private enterprise.

The Subsidies

Sir,—How few appear to realise that subsidies veil the real cost of living. Apparently all's well so long as we can buy eggs at 2d. each, and bread, butter, meat, potatoes, etc., cost us only a fraction of their values. I suggest that the seriousness of the position would be brought home to the public if subsidies were abolished, and they bought articles at their real prices. This would tend to make them more careful with food, less prone to dump the little valued bread, etc., in the pig-bins, and vastly increase the interest in allotments.

This could be offset by a reduction of Income Tax, which is so irritating to the worker. Above all it would kill the Black Market, and the worker would know why he is called upon to work harder and more regularly.
—Yours, etc., OBSERVER.
Birmingham 16

The Prime Minister, the Rt. Hon. Clement Attlee, receives the Freedom of the city, Town Hall, 18th October 1947.

Bull Street, October 1947.

COAL IS THE KEY

The Production Drive for greater exports can't start without MORE COAL!

WE'VE GOT TO GET IT — AND QUICKLY!

ISSUED BY THE NATIONAL COAL BOARD

John Cheesman (right) and Robin Clarke, both originally enrolled as Bevin Boys, Jubilee Colliery, Hamstead, c 1947.

Jubilee Colliery Mine's Rescue Team, on a training course, in Dudley, 1947. The two men, not kitted up, are their instructors.

CITY OF BIRMINGHAM   CONSUMER'S COPY **2A**

COAL DISTRIBUTION ORDER, 1943

NOTIFICATION OF REGISTRATION OF CONTROLLED PREMISES WITH A LICENSED MERCHANT

To   Mr. E. Broadbent.,

Plot 4, Colleen Avenue,   Date 22nd Oct. 1947.

off Penlins Way., Kings Norton. 30.

BIRMINGHAM

I hereby notify you that your registration with the undermentioned merchant in respect of fuel supplies to the above premises has been duly completed.   Depot:- Kings Norton.

A copy of this notice has been forwarded to your registered merchant :—

Messrs A. E. Richardson.,

167, Park Rd., Hockley,   (725)

Birmingham. 18.

You must purchase all your fuel requirements from your registered merchant unless permission to transfer registration has been granted by the Local Fuel Overseer. Failure to observe these provisions renders you liable to penalties under the Defence Regulations.

CIVIC CENTRE,
BIRMINGHAM, 1   Examined by   A. E. GILBERT,
Local Fuel Overseer.

P466—B5—K

The crowds leave Bromford Races, c 1947.

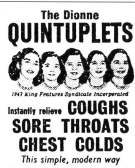

PRINCESS'S THANKS TO BIRMINGHAM

The Lord Mayor of Birmingham has received the following letter of thanks signed by Princess Elizabeth:

BUCKINGHAM PALACE,
16th November, 1947.

My Lord Mayor.

The magnificent silver tea service which the City of Birmingham has sent me is an object of admiration to all who have seen it, and it would be difficult for me to exaggerate the pleasure which this Wedding Present has given me.

The world wide reputation for silver which Birmingham has long enjoyed is certainly upheld in this service, and I can assure you that Lieutenant Mountbatten and I are delighted with it.

Whenever we use it, which will be often, it will remind us of the generosity of the people of Birmingham and of the good wishes which we know that they send us at this very happy period in our lives.

Yours sincerely,
(Signed) ELIZABETH.

New Street, looking across to High Street, 1947.

Albert Place, Friston Street, Ladywood, December 1947.

710 Coventry Road, Small Heath, 2nd December 1947.

Rear of Hospital Street, Hockley, 9th December 1947.

The Lord Mayor, Coun. John Burman, pays a visit to the ex-servicemen's canteen, Windmill Street,
8th December 1947.

On Air Force leave, Norman Bailey
dances with his sister, Lily, Tower
Ballroom, December 1947.

Last minute shopping in the Bull Ring, Christmas Eve 1947.

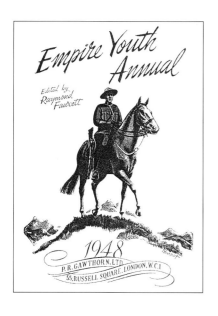

Bridge players, involved in the International Tournament, meet the Lord Mayor and Lady Mayoress, Coun. and Mrs John Burman, and their daughter, Rosanne, 28th February 1948.

Hospital Street, Hockley, 1948.

Macdonald Street, Highgate, February 1948.

The retiring Midland Regional Director of the BBC, Percy Edgar, is presented with a motor lawn mower at the BBC Club, Broad Street, 8th April 1948. He was known to a generation of listening children as "Uncle Percy".

Vic Oliver, usually seen as a comedian and violinist, conducts the British Concert Orchestra, Hippodrome, 25th April 1948.

THESE are a few of the many handsome postage stamps issued in the Commonwealth and Empire during the past two years. Unfortunately we cannot show them in their full colours, as this is not allowed by the G.P.O. The Hong Kong Victory issue (29-8-46) is brown and red ; that of Malta (8-6-46) is blue, as are the Jamaica (20-8-46) and Barbados (1-4-47) issues. Of the three Royal Visit issues, that of Southern Rhodesia (1-4-47) is scarlet and black ; Swaziland (17-2-47) scarlet ; and South Africa (17-2-47) blue. The New Zealand Health issue (24-10-46) is green and orange-brown ; the Australian Mitchell Centenary (14-10-46) grey-olive ; the Falkland Is. (10-12-46) scarlet and black ; and the Dependencies (11-2-46) black and claret.

Barrow's Self-Service Restaurant, Corporation Street, 1948.

Barrow's Despatch Warehouse, Dalton Street, 1948.

Spiceal Street, 1948.

The King and Queen visit the British Industries Fair, Castle Bromwich, 11th May 1948...

... and on to examine a patent food container...

... and finally to the ICI stand for another demonstration.

The King and Queen meet some of the children and wounded ex-servicemen, outside the Town Hall,
11th May 1948.

The King and Queen's departure from the Council House, 11th May 1948.

The crowds converge on the Royal cavalcade as it travels slowly along Corporation Street, 11th May 1948.

Dame Elizabeth Cadbury with the May
Queen, Jean Ridgewell, Bournville fete,
1948.

The Rt. Hon. James Griffiths, M.P.
MINISTER OF NATIONAL INSURANCE

THE 5th July 1948 will be a great day in the development of
our British Social Services. On that day we shall see
National Insurance, including Industrial Injury Insurance, in
full operation, supporting—and supported by—Family Allowances, the National Health Service and National Assistance. We
have indeed come a long way from the Old Age Pensions Act of
1908 (which gave the 5s. a week pension at 70), to this new
system of Social Security which provides help for childbirth, in
sickness, in unemployment, in bereavement, and in old age.

The system will provide for everybody without exception: men,
women and children, young and old, rich and poor, married and
single, employer and employed, those working on their own
account, and those not working at all.

This booklet tells you how much you must pay each week and
what benefits you will receive in return. It is not possible, of
course, to set out all the details in such a short guide, and I am
afraid you will find some parts complicated, and perhaps
difficult to apply to yourself. If you are in doubt on any point
please ask your nearest National Insurance Office for help.
You will find the staff there very ready to give you all the
help and explanation they can.

The success of this great Insurance Scheme depends upon the
willing co-operation of every one of us. Our benefits must be
paid for out of our contributions and our taxes. This scheme is,
therefore, more than an Act of Parliament; it is an act of faith
in the British people. That faith, I know, is not misplaced.

James Griffiths

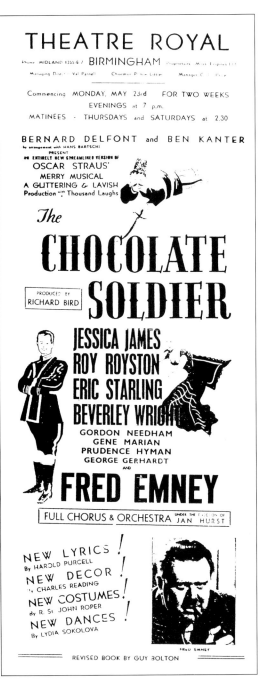

Martineau Street/Bull Street, June 1948.

White Hart, Tile Cross Road, c 1948.

Joan McFarland (left) and friend, successfully recovering from TB, West Heath Sanatorium, 1948. Yes, you are right about those banjoes!

S.A.E.C.
V.A. CAMP
ILTON

A group of Midlanders, including several people from Birmingham, at an agricultural camp at Yeovil, Summer 1948.

Corporation Street, 14th July 1948.

Limberlost Tennis Club, Handsworth Wood, c 1948.

Yardley Road, Acocks Green, c 1948.

Ald. Albert Bradbeer opens the Mobile Safety First Exhibition, Civic Centre, 16th August 1948.

Great Francis Street/Clarendon Street, Vauxhall, c 1948.

Camp Hill, 1948.

Thomas Street/Adelaide Street/Macdonald Street, Highgate, 1948.

Co-op Dairy Manager, Mr Procter, (second right) presents a
cheque to Eric Hollies, as a result of the Benefit Match.
10th September 1948. The Warwickshire captain,
Tom Dollery, is on the left.

Phone
BEArwood 2880.

155, POPLAR AVENUE,
EDGBASTON,
BIRMINGHAM 17.

Sept 15th 1948

Statement of Fees.

To NEVILLE RAYNER,

MUS. BAC.

Pianoforte Playing	Elementary	3 gns
	Moderate	3½ gns
	Advanced	4 gns
Harmony etc.	And all	
Exam. Coaching	Theoretical Subjects	3 gns.
Music		

Total   £

For a Term of 10 lessons beginning over a 12 weekly period.
ALL FEES PAYABLE IN ADVANCE.

St Martin's Church, from Moat Row,
29th November 1948.

Staff party, Royalty Cinema, High Street, Harborne, Christmas 1948.

Gothic Arcade, Snow Hill, c 1949.

A temporary car park, opposite the Odeon, New Street, January 1949.

THE NEW
HUMBER HAWK

A FULL SIX-SEATER...ROOMY BUT COMPACT
...POWERFUL BUT ECONOMICAL

Beautiful wide streamlined bodies
Independent coil spring front suspension
Bench-type front seat
Proved Synchromatic gear control
Exceptional covered luggage accommodation
New "Opticurve" windscreen

A PRODUCT OF THE ROOTES GROUP

HARBORNE MOTORS
YORK STREET, HARBORNE
Phone: 3056

Mrs Florence Thursfield in the kitchen of her
home in Brunswick Road, Handsworth, c 1949.
If you needed a single image, to best represent
domestic life in the forties, this would have
to be a contender.

A happy example of co-operation between management and workers comes to-day from the Cyclo Gear Company, of Potters Hill, Aston—where the above picture was taken—75 per cent. of whose output of cycle gears and cycle accessories is exported to 55 different countries. Te 120 men and 130 women employed by this firm are working voluntaily a 62½-hour week instead of the usual 47½-hour week, and at normal piecework rates. It was their own idea to help with a very full order book. "It involves starting at 7.30 a.m. and finishing at 8 p.m.," said Mr. Edwin Camillis, the firm's works manager. "It means, of course, that we can get bigger production for the same overheads." Despite increased prices of raw materials, and other higher costs, the firm, by means of co-operation with the workers and bigger outputs, has contrived to keep the prices of its goods down to the 1942 level.

Toolroom, Cyclo Gear Co. Ltd., Aston, 1949.

Icknield Street, looking towards Warstone Lane, 4th February 1949.

The Birmingham Eagles Roller Speed Skating Club, Embassy Sportsdrome, Walford Road, Sparkhill, 1949.

Operatic singer and actor, Paul Robeson, acknowledges the welcome from the waiting crowd, Town Hall, 25th February 1949.

Cadbury Bros. Ltd., Bournville, February 1949.

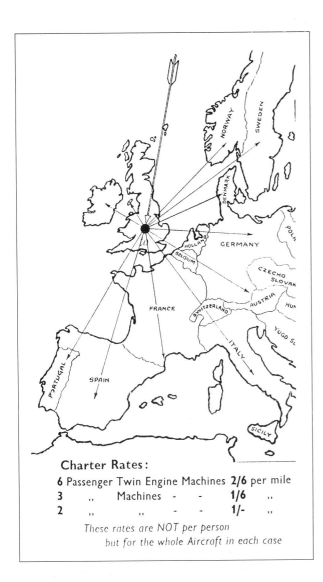

Charter Rates:

6 Passenger Twin Engine Machines **2/6** per mile
3   ,,   Machines - -   **1/6**   ,,
2   ,,   ,,   - -   **1/-**   ,,

*These rates are NOT per person
but for the whole Aircraft in each case*

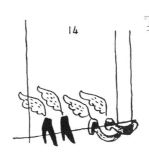

Lord Pakenham, Minister of Civil Aviation, prepares to open
the first international service from Birmingham by BEA, to
Paris, 8th April 1949. He is now known as Lord Longford.

Sutherland Street, Aston, 1949.

Navigation Street, c 1949.

Navigation Street/Hill Street, 12th April 1949.

The junction of Suffolk Street and John Bright Street, 1949.

Proving once again the popularity of Royal visits,
as the crowds turn out to greet Princess Elizabeth and the
Duke of Edinburgh, Victoria Square, 10th May 1949.

The Firm have engaged for the Cadbury programme Britain's No. 1 film star, John Mills. Each Sunday night from 9.30 to 10 p.m. he broadcasts a programme called "A Goodnight Story," in which the works of famous short

John Mills at the microphone

story writers are presented in dramatised form. The following are among the well-known works already broadcast : *The Purple Pileus* (H. G. Wells), *Family Cares* (W. W. Jacobs), *Sire de Maletroit* (R. L. Stevenson), *The Kite* (Somerset Maugham), *The White Pony* (H. E. Bates) and *The Canterville Ghost* (Oscar Wilde).

The growing popularity of John Mills and the Cadbury programme is very evident from the ever-increasing fan-mail which arrives at Bournville each week.

Many people in the Birmingham area find it difficult to get first-class reception from Luxembourg, but the transmitter strength is rapidly improving. We recommend "A Goodnight Story" as a very pleasant entertainment to round off Sunday's listening. It advertises Bourn-vita as the "goodnight" food drink.

Luxembourg's wave length is 1,293 metres.

FINAL LEAGUE POSITIONS 1948-49

LEAGUE I

	Pld.	Won	Drn.	Lost	GOALS For	Agst.	Pts.
Portsmouth.	42	25	8	9	84	42	58
Manchester United	42	21	11	10	77	44	53
Derby County	42	22	9	11	74	55	53
Newcastle United	42	20	12	10	70	56	52
Arsenal	42	18	13	11	74	44	49
Wolver'ton Wanderers	42	17	12	13	79	66	46
Manchester City	42	15	15	12	47	51	45
Sunderland.	42	13	17	12	49	58	43
Charlton	42	15	12	15	63	67	42
Aston Villa.	42	16	10	16	60	76	42
Stoke	42	16	9	17	66	68	41
Liverpool	42	13	14	15	53	43	40
Chelsea	42	12	14	16	69	68	38
Burnley	42	12	14	15	43	50	38
Bolton Wanderers.	42	14	10	18	59	68	38
Blackpool	42	11	16	15	54	67	38
Birmingham City	42	11	15	16	36	38	37
Everton	42	13	11	18	41	63	37
Middlesbrough	42	11	12	19	46	57	34
Huddersfield	42	12	10	20	40	69	34
Preston	42	11	11	20	62	75	33
Sheffield United.	42	11	11	20	57	78	33

Heneage Street, Aston, 1949.

Harborne Lane, Harborne, May 1949.

The first bus to be painted in the new British Railway colours, 12th May 1949. It was to convey relief train crews from Saltley to various local stations.

Midland Red Beauty Queen, Rosalind Allen, with her ladies-in-waiting and the competition judges, at the Annual Sports' Day, 5th July 1949.

Easy Row, 1949.

Benson Road Elementary School, Soho, c 1949.

Dr G.T. Warwick (2nd right) and a party of geography students from the University of Birmingham, on expedition to the Arctic Circle of Norway, 1949.

Contestants from Turves Green Secondary Modern School prepare to leave, from New Street Station, for Stockholm, to represent England in the world gymnastics' festival, July 1949.

No parking problems for the Bond car, Waterloo Street, 1949.

Monument Road/Reservoir Road, Ladywood, September 1949.

Palais de Danse, Monument Road, Edgbaston, c 1949.

Oaktree Lane/Bristol Road, Selly Oak, 1949.

Chamberlain Square, 23rd September 1949.

Montgomery Street, Small Heath,
23rd November 1949.

War-damaged furniture at Cambridge Street stores,
1949.

More and more miles are proving

AUSTIN

—you can depend on it!

Current Austins comprise 8, 10, 12 and 16 h.p. de-luxe, 4-door, 4-cylinder sliding head saloons, priced from £280 to £525. Also the 'A110' Sheerline and 'A120' Princess 6-cylinder saloons, priced at £999 and £1,350 respectively. *All the above prices are subject to Purchase Tax.*

TWO CENTURIES MILESTONE
at Kirkstall in Yorkshire. This stone is 200 miles from the capital of Scotland and 200 from the capital of England.

THE AUSTIN MOTOR CO LTD • LONGBRIDGE • BIRMINGHAM

AL SHARKEY FORMS OWN QUARTET

Appearing each Wednesday and Saturday at the Moorpool Ballroom, Harborne, is a quartet led by trumpeter Al Sharkey, who recently left Musical Direction (Vincent Ladbrook's office) to launch out as a leader in his own right.

Pamela Venn now with Sonny Rose

Nineteen-year-old Pamela Venn, now singing with Sonny Rose and his Band at the West End Ballroom, Birmingham, began her career as a vocalist at the age of 14. She was introduced in "Opportunity Knocks" by Birmingham University band-leader Allan Ayres in June last.

The Birmingham & Midland Motor Omnibus Co. Ltd.

LOST PROPERTY

BEARWOOD GARAGE 4314

Handed in by Conductor *A. Ramsbottom*

Date Found *30/11/49* Time Found *4-10 a.m. p.m.* Bus No. *2222*

ROUTE *Dudley Zoo* Service No. *125*

Full Description of Property *One gents umbrella, black, with horse-head handle*

Date handed in *30/11/49* Received by (Clerk) *S. Holloway*

This portion to be affixed to article

B. & M.N.
LOST P
CONDUCTOR'S RECEIPT

BEARWOOD GARAGE 4314

This portion must be detached by Cash Clerk and returned to Conductor only AFTER receipt of article.

"LUCKILY, IT WAS ONLY A BOTTLE OF YOUR OLD BRANDY"

It's a "lucky break" for everyone with H.P. on the table as usual. The delicious flavour stimulates appetite — ensures the enjoyment that makes meals more nourishing.

HP SAUCE

HAYFIELD'S *for*

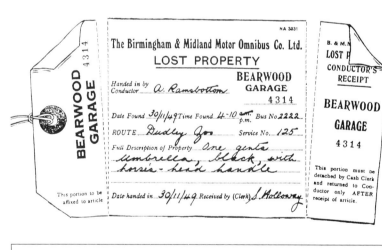

HOUSEHOLD REMOVALS

LARGE OR SMALL

LOCAL OR LONG DISTANCE SPECIALISTS

★

Call, write or phone
BEArwood 1064
for immediate estimates

365 BEARWOOD ROAD, SMETHWICK
(Next to Windsor Theatre)

and 63 STANLEY AVENUE, HARBORNE, 32
(1 min. Odeon, Warley)   Phone : BEA 2503

PASS THE MUSTARD PLEASE

Mustard and meat were made for each other . . . Mustard whets appetite, sharpens flavour and spurs digestion.

It's nicer with COLMAN'S MUSTARD

118

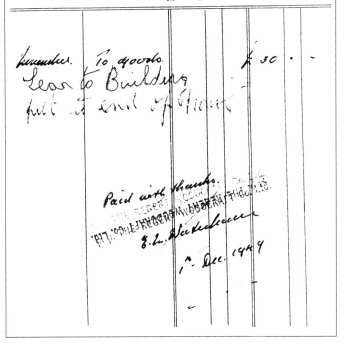

Carol Service, St Martin's Church,
22nd December 1949.

Bordesley Street, 30th December 1949.

Back Cover: Louis de Camillis, the founder of Cyclo Gear Co. Ltd., of Aston, complete with gas mask, Barr Beacon, April 1941. This might be a good idea for cyclists today, to combat pollution!

ACKNOWLEDGEMENTS

(for providing photographs, for encouragement and numerous other favours)

Norman Bailey; The late Dorothy Bevan; The Birmingham City Council Dept. of Planning and Architecture; Birmingham International Airport; The Birmingham Post and Mail Ltd.; Hilda Broadbent; Anne Cannell; Dave and Kath Carpenter; John Cheesman; Annette Dickers; Eddystone Radio Ltd.; John Enticknap; Peter Fletcher; Joyce Gill; Robin and Elaine Harriott; George and Jeanette Holt; John Hotchkiss; The International Print Shop (Kings Norton Green); Anne Jennings; Thelma Jones; Jim Kendall; Joyce Lockwood; Millie Mills; Dennis Moore; George Peace; David Perrins; Rex Preece; Douglas Price; Clyde Riley; Travel West Midlands; The University of Birmingham; Andy Wade; Joan Wanty; Joan Ward; Ron While; Rosemary Wilkes.

Please forgive any possible omissions. Every effort has been made to include all organisations and individuals involved in the book.

Princess Elizabeth and the Duke of Edinburgh receive a regal bow from Michael Burman, Stechford Station, 10th May 1949.